I0455594

CONTENTS

Foreword vii

1. Introduction 1
    Stephen J. Blank

2. How the U.S. Withdrawal from Afghanistan
    Will Affect Russia and Eurasia 13
    Ariel Cohen

3. Collusive Status-Seeking: The Sino-Russian
    Relationship 33
    Geir Flikke

4. China's Military Goals, Policy, Doctrine,
    and Capabilities in Central Asia 81
    Richard Weitz

About the Contributors 123

CHAPTER 1

INTRODUCTION

Stephen J. Blank

The papers collected here were presented at the Fourth annual Strategic Studies Institute (SSI) conference on Russia in May 2012. They focus largely, though not exclusively, on the interactions of the great powers in, about, and around Central Asia. That said, it is imperative that anyone trying to make sense of the complex situation in Central Asia remember that the contemporary or new great game is not played upon a chessboard of inert Central Asian subjects, as was the case in Kipling's time. Today the Central Asian states are all active subjects, as well as objects of international action, and are perfectly capable of attempting, even successfully, to shape the interactions of great powers and foreign institutions upon their politics.[1] As a result, today's version of the new great game is a multidimensional and multiplayer game that is played simultaneously on many "chessboards."

Furthermore, that game is about to change dramatically and substantively. The United States and the North Atlantic Treaty Organization (NATO) have already begun preparations to withdraw from Afghanistan. Beyond that, U.S. funding for Central Asia as a whole, probably in anticipation of long-term constrained budgets, has also begun to fall.[2] Since U.S. strategy in Central Asia has been officially presented as essentially an adjunct to the war in Afghanistan, these emerging trends oblige the United States to formulate a new, less militarily-oriented strategy for the entire region—one that sees the region simultaneously in both its integrity and diversity. For many reasons, doing so will present a difficult challenge to U.S. military-political leaders. These difficulties include the actions of external players like Russia and China, among others, and are not confined solely to U.S. interaction with Central Asia. Indeed, as the papers included here show, the complexities of foreign interaction with Central Asia are both intensifying and accelerating, obligating the United States to realign its regional strategy and policy.

That strategy has been primarily focused on the military requirements of defeating the Taliban as a prelude to winning the war in Afghanistan. That outcome would, in turn, serve as the basis for stabilizing Afghanistan internally and then providing for the stabilization of the adjacent states of Central Asia, whose regional cooperation with Afghanistan is vital to its security and theirs after 2014.[3] These states possess limited resources with which to help bring Afghanistan to a more secure condition after 2014, though they are making contributions to that end. However, the impending drawdown of NATO's International Security Assistance Force (ISAF) and U.S. forces, plus widespread skepticism as to the staying power of the Karzai regime after that drawdown, repeatedly leads their governments to warn that Afghanistan's and their future is, to some degree, at considerable risk.[4] While some of these statements are fearmongering to increase pressure upon foreign donors to assist them, their fears are real enough, and they are certainly not groundless.

At present, it is clear that the U.S. military is planning to leave some forces behind, though the precise number and status of those forces is as yet undecided, and it is difficult to imagine the United States simply

2

turning over five large air bases to Afghanistan. The Pentagon and the government are also busy setting up training and advisory facilities with Central Asian governments. As the U.S. Central Command (US-CENTCOM) 2013 Posture Statement states:

> Coupled with our NDN [Northern Distribution Network] efforts, USCENTCOM will continue to provide military assistance focused on building partner capacity and capabilities to combat terrorists and counter illegal trafficking in all its forms. In addition, we will work closely with several of our willing partners who are committed to developing deployable peacekeeping units. Programs and authorities such as Section 1206 [Global Train and Equip Fund] and the new Global Security Contingency Fund, together with the National Guard's State Partnership Program [SPP] represent cost-effective means for the United States to respond to emerging opportunities for building partner capacity.[5]

There is also a widespread assumption that if Kyrgyzstan terminates the U.S. lease upon the Manas Air Base in 2014, the United States has a so-called "Plan B" up its sleeve, namely the establishment of a military base or rapid response center in Uzbekistan that would permit a U.S. presence, though of undisclosed size, in Central Asia and give Uzbekistan added leverage against Russian pressure to subordinate Uzbekistan to Russian preferences.[6] Indeed, many Central Asian governments have approached the United States for bases for precisely this purpose, as well as for defense against the Taliban since 2001, but to no avail.[7] Moreover, there is an equally widespread expectation of a future civil war outside of the U.S. military command and a gathering number of critiques of a U.S. strategy that critics feel has been misconceived for a long time.[8]

Thus, since 2001, U.S. military strategists have treated this region solely as a geographic and occasionally political obstacle to operations — something to be transited or crossed en route to or from Afghanistan. In accordance with the current strategy, when OEF [Operation ENDURING FREEDOM] ends, U.S. operational requirements in the region will also end, and Central Asia will cease to be of concern. Current U.S. military strategy in Central Asia is best summarized as 'do whatever is necessary to keep our bases and supply routes open until the last U.S. soldier leaves Afghanistan in 2014.' As important as it is to support the war fighters in OEF, the problem with this approach is that it fails to acknowledge the strategic significance of the Central Asian region in its own right. A strategic analysis of the region demonstrates that Afghanistan and Central Asia are inextricably linked, strategically as well as operationally. Strategic success in Central Asia is critical to strategic (not just operational) success in Afghanistan, and vice versa.[9]

Yet at the same time, these states' requests for a U.S. presence, military or otherwise, trigger widespread fears among major powers like Russia and China that the United States is seeking to establish some sort of military protectorate or sphere of influence in the region or to balance or even oust them. Since local states, like all other Third World governments, are exceedingly sensitive to anything that even remotely looks like "neo-colonialism," reports of these facilities in their media frequently trigger exactly the same accusations against U.S. policies, not only in Moscow or in Beijing, but also among some Central Asian regimes.[10] Alternatively, a sizable U.S. presence could attract Taliban attention and make a state like Uzbekistan a target of both military and political action against the current regime and that accompanying U.S. presence.[11] In that case, indigenous Uzbek anti-regime elements or Uzbek and other Central Asian terrorists affiliated with the Taliban and/or al-Qaeda could then use Afghanistan as a springboard for such attacks. Simultaneously, Russia and China are not only pouring resources of their own into Central Asia, but they are also trying to set up binding arrangements that would, in fact, subordinate those governments to their regional and genuinely neo-colonial aspirations in this part of the world. Geir Flikke's and Richard Weitz's papers clearly show this pattern of increased capability to project influence into Central Asia, a heightened sensitivity and rivalry between them concerning each other's activities here, and simultaneously their joint and united opposition to any sign of an enhanced U.S. presence, especially a military one.

Moreover, as budget constraints take hold and will do so for years to come, it will be increasingly difficult for the U.S. Government and any of the U.S. forces, but especially the Army, to maintain a credible and enduring strategic presence in Central Asia since military bases clearly provide a major entrée for the United States into Central Asia.[12] The absence of a coherent U.S. strategy or resources or truly sustainable presence in Central Asia greatly impedes the possibility of deploying the kinds of forces that the Army wants to build, i.e., an Army that is "globally engaged and capable of rapidly employing scalable force packages from the smallest to the largest depending on the demands of the situation."[13] Under such circumstances, at least as far as potential future crises in Central Asia are concerned, it will also become progressively more difficult, if not beyond American capabilities, to adhere to the injunctions of key U.S. strategy documents

5

insofar as they pertain to this region. Thus the Army's *Capstone Concept of 2012* states that:

> The Army must maintain a credible, robust capacity to win decisively and the depth and resilience to support combatant commanders across the range of military operations in the homeland and abroad.[14]

Similarly, the *2010 National Security Strategy* states:

> We will continue to rebalance our military capabilities to excel at counterterrorism, counterinsurgency, stability operations, and meeting increasingly sophisticated security threats, while ensuring our force is ready to address the full range of military operations.[15]

Under conditions of withering financial stringency that have only just begun, and given the foreseeable strategic realities in Central Asia, including Afghanistan, in 2014, and the wisdom embodied in Frederick the Great's timeless admonition that he who seeks to defend against everything ends by defending nothing, it is hard to see exactly how the United States thinks it can project and sustain military force into Central Asia for any length of time after 2014 if necessary and to what kind of coherent strategic purpose it can do so.

Under these circumstances, and assuming that we still think Central Asia is of sufficient strategic importance to pursue strategic interests there by direct force, the endlessly reiterated Army argument that the Army must be ready for operations that span the entire range of military operations is a recipe for deploying a force capable only of tactical proficiency at the expense of strategic insight and capability.[16] In fact, all we may be capable of sustaining in Central

Asia is a robust security assistance program. While that concept is moving to the fore under combined fiscal and strategic realities, it also implies that should there be another major crisis there, we might have to walk away because we lack the capability to project and sustain credible forces in that theater or for lack of a definable vital interest.[17] Arguably, statements or policies implying that not only will the United States remain in Central Asia but that it can also prepare for and sustain forces capable of spanning the whole range of military operations there are, in the current fiscal and political climate, the antithesis of strategic thinking and literally inconceivable. This is another way of saying that, absent the investment and/or sponsorship of other parties' investments in Central Asia and Afghanistan after 2014, commensurate with the region's real challenges that are largely economic and political in character, neither the U.S. military nor the government has a viable strategy for the area.[18] Neither private U.S. organizations nor the U.S. Government are investing nearly enough to reckon with those economic political challenges, and talk of the Silk Road remains just that—talk, since the funding for it is not being allocated.[19]

While U.S. Army programs probably should concentrate after 2014 on enhancing security cooperation in all its multifarious forms, as described in the literature on the subject, with Central Asian militaries that are willing to do so, the real issue is whether the administration and Congress will make a formal policy decision, as embodied not in rhetoric but in actual allocations and policies, that a robust and multidimensional private and public U.S. presence in Central Asia is in America's vital interest. Central Asian governments value the U.S. presence highly and want it to continue. They certainly want more investment or use of Washington's power to convene and leverage other institutions, be they private, public, or multilateral, to invest in key sectors like infrastructure, transportation, water, and communications. Those are among the real deeply rooted challenges to security in Central Asia and are sectors where U.S. and other foreign investments could make a real difference.

But for that kind of outcome to ensue, Washington must make it clear to both domestic and foreign interlocutors that it considers Central Asia a critical zone and vigorously intends to sustain its presence there. And that is not happening.[20] The failure to do so will only stimulate local governments to continue to be anti-liberal and repressive, if not incapable of contending with their massive governance challenges. This failure will also leave a vacuum behind that Moscow and Beijing will try to fill. Others like India, Pakistan, Iran, and even possibly Turkey will also try to do so, but they will be handicapped relative to the governments of Russia and China because of their own relative weakness and/or absence of a viable U.S. presence. Therefore, the issue confronting the U.S. Government as a whole, and its armed forces in particular, is not the relevance of Landpower. As far as Central Asia is concerned, we neither have the resources nor the manpower to engage in a sustained long-term ground campaign there. Thus, we do not have sufficiently credible Landpower as far as Central Asian strategic outcomes are concerned. Rather, the issue is determining the extent to which Washington regards Central Asia as a critical or vital strategic region and the extent of its willingness to commit resources to implement its strategic vision or persuade others to do so in tandem with it. This should not be fundamentally a question

8

of defense policy, though the space of enhanced security cooperation will be a key military component of that policy in peacetime, if not during local wars, unless Central Asia falls apart. Rather, the challenge is to see Central Asia as vital in its own right, not as an adjunct to Afghanistan or some other strategic design.

Since the administration has not yet accepted that Central Asia may be vital to U.S. interests and is already diminishing the resources necessary to sustain any such vision, its resources with which to execute such a strategically oriented program of action will necessarily be limited. Moreover, it is also clear that the real challenges here are not military, and it is highly unlikely that we will send combat forces into this area again, barring a major threat to the United States and its acknowledged vital interests. It therefore becomes critical for agencies who must conduct policies here to leverage those scarce resources that are or will be available by enhancing their understanding of regional socioeconomic-political dynamics and recognizing that the fundamental challenges to regional security originate in those dynamics and not in military responses that are maladapted for responding to those problems. Hopefully, the essays collected here will contribute to that understanding.

ENDNOTES - CHAPTER 1

1. Alexander Cooley, *Great Games, Local Rules: The New Great Power Contest in Central Asia*, New York: Oxford University Press, 2012, is the most cogent recent statement of that fact.

2. Stephen Blank, *Central Asian Perspectives on Afghanistan After the US Withdrawal*, Afghanistan Regional Forum, No. 2, Washington, DC: Central Asia Program, 2012.

3. Vali Nasr, *The Dispensable Nation: American Foreign Policy in Retreat*, New York: Doubleday, 2013.

4. Blank, *Central Asian Perspectives*.

5. Statement of General James N. Mattis (USMC), Commander, United States Central Command (USCENTCOM), before the Senate Armed Services Committee on the posture of U.S. Central Command, March 5, 2013, p. 22, available from *www.senate.gov*.

6. Jacob Zenn, "What Options for U.S. Influence in Central Asia After Manas?" *Central Asia Caucasus Analyst*, March 6, 2013.

7. Joshua Kucera, "Tajikistan Wanted U.S. Air Base At Kulyab; Rumsfeld Gave Them Bridge Instead," *Eurasia Insight*, March 15, 2013; Ahmed Rashid, "Security vs. Reconciliation: The Afghan Conundrum," *New York Review of Books Blog*, February 13, 2012, available from *www.nybooks.com/blogs/*; Erica Marat, "After Winning Elections Atambayev Focuses on the US Transit Center," *Eurasia Daily Monitor*, November 3, 2011; Bishkek, *Kyrgyz Television 1*, in Kyrgyz, May 2, 2012, *Foreign Broadcast Information Service-Soviet (FBIS-SOV)*, May 2, 2012.

8. Dexter Filkins, "After America," *The New Yorker*, July 9 and 16, 2002, pp. 54-67; Lewis G. Irwin, *Disjointed Ways, Disunified Means: Learning From America's Struggle to Build an Afghan Nation*, Carlisle, PA: Strategic Studies Institute, U.S. Army War College, 2012.

9. Ted Donnelly, *Fergana as FATA? Central Asia after 2014 – Outcomes and Strategic Options*, Ft. Leavenworth, KS: Foreign Military Studies Office, 2011, p. 6.

10. See, for example, Parviz Mullojonov, "USA's Strategy: A New Silk Road—Road to Nowhere," Dushanbe, *Avesta*, in Russian, February 21, 2013, *Open Source Center, FBIS SOV*, February 21, 2013.

11. Zenn.

12. *Ibid.*

13. General Raymond T. Odierno (USA), "The Force of Tomorrow," *Foreign Policy*, February 4, 2013, available from *www.foreignpolicy.com*.

14. *The U.S. Army Capstone Concept*, Ft. Leavenworth, KS: U.S. Army Training and Doctrine Command (TRADOC), 2012, p. 24.

15. *National Security Strategy*, Washington, DC: The White House, 2010, p. 14, available from *www.whitehouse.gov*.

16. General Raymond T. Odierno, "The U.S. Army in a Time of Transition," *Foreign Affairs* May-June, 2012, available from *www.foreignaffairs. com/articles/137423/raymond-t-odierno/the-us-army-in-a-time-of-transition*; U.S. Army, *2012 Strategic Planning Guidance*, available from *www.army.mil/ standto/archive/issue.php?issue=2012-04-27; Pamphlet 525-3-1, The United States Army Operating Concept 2016-2028*, Washington, DC: TRADOC, 2010; *Pamphlet 525-3-0, The Army Capstone Concept: Operational Adaptability: Operating Under Conditions of Uncertainty and Complexity in an Era of Persistent Conflict*, Washington, DC: TRADOC, 2009; *2012 Strategic Planning Guidance*, Washington, DC: U.S. Army, 2012.

17. John A. Nagl, "In an Era of Small Wars, U.S. Army Must Embrace Training Mission," *World Politics Review*, February 5, 2013; Daniel Wasserbly, "Panetta Seeks Investments in Regional Engagement, Partner Capacity," *Jane's Defence Weekly*, December 20, 2012, available from *www.ihs.com/products/janes/defence-business/news/defence-weekly.aspx*.

18. Blank, *Central Asia Perspectives*; S. Frederick Starr *et al.*, *Finish the Job: Jump-Start Afghanistan's Economy: A Handbook of Projects*, Washington, DC, and Stockholm, Sweden: Central Asia Caucasus Institute, Silk Road Studies Program, Johns Hopkins University and the Institute for Security and Development Policy, 2012; Stephen Blank, "How Durable and Sustainable is Indo-American Cooperation in South and Central Asia?" paper presented to the SSI-Dickinson College Conference Cross-Sector Collaboration to Promote Sustainable Development, Carlisle, PA, March 13, 2013.

19. *Ibid.*

20. *Ibid.*

CHAPTER 2

HOW THE U.S. WITHDRAWAL FROM AFGHANISTAN WILL AFFECT RUSSIA AND EURASIA

Ariel Cohen

Anton A. Altman, the Heritage Foundation intern, contributed greatly to production of this chapter.

As the United States is planning for its withdrawal from Afghanistan, regional actors are re-evaluating the strategic environment and have begun planning for the future. For Russia today, Afghanistan is both a painful memory and a threat to its desired regional dominance in Central Asia. Memories of the Soviet Union's 10-year war in Afghanistan have yet to fade and still weigh heavily on the Russian conscience. The U.S. opinion makers actively avoid drawing the parallels between the Soviet military engagement more than 2 decades ago and the current struggle to stabilize Afghanistan. The Soviets left with the ill-fated Najibullah regime in place, and the North Atlantic Treaty Organization (NATO) plans to have an arrangement in Kabul that will look like a defeat. Russia's complex web of relationships with Afghan parties (especially the Tajiks and the Uzbeks, who controlled the Northern Alliance), with Afghanistan's neighboring states, and with the West will therefore play a significant role in the outcome of NATO involvement in Afghanistan.

THE VIEW FROM THE NORTH

In July 2011, Russia witnessed the first U.S. troops beginning their withdrawal from Afghanistan and the West's determination to cede security responsibilities over to the Afghan National Security Forces (ANSF). The withdrawal, planned to be completed by 2014, has put the issue of an independent Afghanistan back on the radar of Central Asian states and regional powers. Afghanistan's neighbors will gain a greater autonomy in their relationship with Kabul, and Russia occupies an important position in this development.

In the aftermath of September 11, 2001 (9/11), Russia stood ready to assist the United States in fighting the Taliban and al-Qaeda. Moscow feared the total control of Afghanistan by Islamist extremists and understood the potential consequences of allowing the situation to draw on, including the threat of escalating violence in Central Asia. However, Russia was wary of engaging its own military. Moscow's assistance amounted to material support and some intelligence sharing with the United States on Afghanistan. Russia chose to consolidate its interests in Central Asia and to allow the United States and NATO to deal with the military threat.

Russia's ill-fated invasion of Afghanistan began when the Soviet Union invaded in 1979 at the height of its power. The ensuing conflict took the lives of 14,300 soldiers, with over 50,000 wounded. Soviet withdrawal came a decade later in 1988-89 as the Soviet Union was crumbling. After the withdrawal, Russia put Afghanistan, and to some extent the Muslim world as a whole, out of its collective conscience for a number of years. This became known as "Afghan Syndrome." It is largely responsible for the intentional exclusion of Central Asian states from the post-Soviet commonwealth in 1991.[1]

What the Russians began to understand from their involvement in Afghanistan was the power of militant Islam and the denominated tribal complexities of the region. As the United States withdraws, Russia fears unrest, chaos, and extremism spreading from Afghanistan north. In the scenario of the Taliban gaining control in Kabul, they expect a spread of radical Islam into Russia's Central Asian neighbors and into territories and groups within Russia itself, such as the North Caucasus. As a result, Moscow fears a diminished influence in its "sphere of privileged interests." A second problem that is bound to escalate in the event of a U.S. failure in Afghanistan is that of drug trafficking. Afghanistan is a large regional producer of opiates that are smuggled not only through, but also into, Russia for consumption by its domestic population. In an Afghanistan without a Western military presence and with an unfriendly government, this problem would be exponentially more difficult to control, despite the often quoted statistic that under the Taliban, fewer opiates were exported than today.

In addition to its complicated relationship with NATO, Russia, along with China, is a founding member of the Shanghai Cooperation Organization (SCO). The SCO concerns itself with Central Asian security. Its goal is to confront the threats of terrorism, separatism, and extremism in Eurasia. Though its actions have been limited, the SCO works on improving military cooperation, intelligence sharing, and counterterrorism.

While it will seek to protect its own interests first and foremost, Russia has a significant role to play in the outcome of Afghanistan's future. Western involvement will be a crucial factor in determining whether or not a stable government exists in Afghanistan down the line. Yet, Russian involvement is boosting the Kabul government, and economic development may also play a positive role. Foreign forces have the unenviable task of striking a balance between hunting down belligerents and not wading too far into Afghanistan's domestic conflict. The endgame for Western involvement must involve an Afghan-run Afghanistan that poses no threat to itself, to its neighbors, and to the West—no easy task.

A Split Personality.

The Kremlin has mixed feelings about the U.S. presence in Afghanistan. Russia is somewhat consoled by the fact that the operation has a United Nations (UN) mandate that Moscow helped draft. Beyond a tepid public support of the international effort to stabilize the situation in Afghanistan, opinions in the political establishment differ. The Russian leadership is wary of the U.S. extended military stay in its own backyard but understands the consequences of a security void in the region. Privately, some in Russia's political leadership would like to see a U.S. failure in Afghanistan reminiscent of the Soviet Union's. This comes purely from a place of anti-Americanism and a false sense of competition.[2]

A pragmatic approach to the situation, however, comes down to the fact that a U.S. failure in Afghanistan would lead to a rise of Islamic radicalism in Afghanistan, and possibly the region, that Russia would not be able to contain. Yet, despite this understanding, the "Afghan Syndrome" holds strong, and Russia has no intention of getting involved militarily in the conflict. Those in Moscow who see the United States as their primary geopolitical adversary would like to see an indefinite U.S. military involvement in Afghanistan with no clear winner. In this scenario, the United States would not allow a Taliban victory but would be tied up in the conflict indefinitely. They favor a spectator policy of very limited assistance to NATO allies in their struggle. This would leave the door open to cutting a deal with the Taliban in the event that becomes necessary after a post-NATO withdrawal. Close ties with the Karzai regime would leave Russia in a weak position, should the current government lose control.

On the other hand, there are those who favor a much closer cooperation with the United States and NATO. Some support for this strategy comes from a "Reset" mindset. If Russia gives the United States support in its time of need, then Moscow will be able to lobby more successfully for issues important to Russia's geopolitical interests. Others support this course of action because of the practical implications. A positive NATO outcome in Afghanistan will benefit the whole region, including Russia's geopolitical interests. A NATO victory would remove the most serious national security threat Russia faces today. This mix of opinions has led to modest Russian support for the U.S. efforts in fighting the Taliban and for the Karzai government.

Moscow's Fears.

Russia views Afghanistan from the perspective of a threat to its regional interests. A militant Islamic power in Afghanistan could lead to a domino effect in the region. That threat could reach as far as Russia's own borders. A Taliban-controlled Kabul regime would encourage Central Asian Islamism and may again offer training camps to Chechen rebels. Moscow fears that the regimes of several countries in the region are not stable enough to handle the stress of such a development and is not confident in its own ability to contain the Taliban's regional influence.

The other, more immediate, problem Russia faces is that of the drugs out of Afghanistan. Recently, this has become a problem of not only trafficking through Russian territory, but also a national epidemic of heroin addiction. According to the UN Office on Drug and Crime (UNODC), Russia has become the world's single largest national market for heroin, consuming approximately 20 percent of all heroin trafficked out of Afghanistan annually.[3] Despite a serious focus on the issue in Moscow, the problem has only gotten worse. There are at least 1.5 million heroin users in Russia, and an estimated 80 people die per day from its use. Since U.S. and Canadian involvement in Afghanistan began in 2001, production levels have reached record levels. According to the Russian government's anti-drug czar, Viktor Ivanov, production in Afghanistan has increased 44 times since the arrival of Western forces in Afghanistan.[4]

The Russian government maintains that the most effective way to solve the problem is to cut it off at the source. In October 2010, Russian and U.S. Special Services collaborated in destroying four Afghan drug laboratories. This was the first collaboration of its kind between the two countries in Afghanistan. In 2010, they also agreed to step up intelligence cooperation on the issue after a Central Intelligence Agency (CIA) report revealed that there were two million heroin addicts living in the United States.[5]

Drugs are smuggled from Afghanistan through Central Asian networks in Uzbekistan, Tajikistan, Kazakhstan, Turkmenistan, and Kyrgyzstan. Russia has had visa free travel with these former Soviet republics since the collapse of the Soviet Union, which may be facilitating traffickers. The special services of the SCO members have suggested that the member states of the SCO (Russia, China, Kazakhstan, Kyrgyzstan, Tajikistan, and Uzbekistan) fight the drug trafficking problem on their own territories, while NATO destroyed the poppy fields prevalent in Afghanistan. NATO has consistently declined to head up the targeting of poppy operations, as this would cause a wave of anti-NATO sentiment.

Russia's drug problem is only liable to get worse in the event of a premature U.S. withdrawal from Afghanistan or if the Taliban come back to power. Without any opposition to drug trafficking within the country, its output is only liable to increase. According to the U.S. House Committee on Foreign Affairs, the Taliban earns $150 million from drug production annually, and total drug profits amount to over $4 billion.[6] This is not a small revenue stream by any means.

Russia has very limited economic interests in Afghanistan. The trade turnover between the two countries in 2008 was just under $200 million.[7] In a 2010 meeting of NATO and Russian chiefs, Russia offered to restore 142 industrial facilities built by Soviet specialists in Afghanistan.[8] This amounted to a hollow gesture, as they requested funding from the international community to complete this work rather than offering assistance for Afghanistan's economic development.

RUSSIA IN INTERNATIONAL SPACE

In *Russia's Strategies in Afghanistan and Their Consequences for NATO*, Marlene Laruelle introduces the following factors as influencing Russia's perspective on Afghanistan:

> In terms of foreign policy, the growing relevance of a long-term strategic rapprochement with western interests against the backdrop of the reconfiguration of powers in the 21st century; in terms of the 'near abroad,' midway between foreign and domestic policy, Moscow's management of its relationship with Central Asia.[9]

In 2001, following the events of 9/11, to the surprise of the Russian military, Vladimir Putin supported the U.S. Intervention in Afghanistan and even acquiesced to the Pentagon opening air bases at Karshi-Khanabad in Uzbekistan and Manas in Kyrgyzstan. Today, the international coalition relies increasingly on Russia for transit. The Northern Distribution Network (NDN), a transport route passing through Russia and its neighbors established in the summer of 2009, carried 40 percent of nonlethal equipment to the International Security Assistance Force (ISAF) in Afghanistan; this amount increased to 75 percent for 2011.[10] Russia also opened up its airspace to the ISAF, as did Kazakhstan at the end of 2010.

Despite its record of assistance to U.S. forces in their operations, Russia remains wary of the U.S. military presence in the neighborhood and has been vocal about its concerns. Russian Foreign Minister Sergei Lavrov has spoken out publicly, objecting to U.S. plans to maintain a presence in Afghanistan following the pullout of international forces in 2014.[11] Another area where Russia's opposition to U.S. presence in the area is apparent is the Manas base in Kyrgyzstan, a key logistics hub. Russia and China regularly lean on Kyrgyz authorities to demand the base's closure. Russia has no real interest in its immediate shutdown, but they use this pressure to send the Pentagon a signal about their distaste for long-term influence of a U.S. military presence in its near abroad.

Russia is far more concerned with the U.S. military presence than the creeping soft power of China in its near abroad. Moscow seems to tolerate the vast economic expansion of China's presence in Central Asia far more than the open-ended U.S. military deployment. Russia has partnered with Beijing to bring the SCO to the international limelight as a forum for discourse, with India, Pakistan, Afghanistan, Mongolia, and Iran as observers. Beijing supports dialogue with "moderate" Taliban groups, while others, such as India, take the hard line of rejecting all negotiation.

Afghanistan is a delicate issue in Russia's relationships with India and Pakistan. India's understanding is that Pakistan's military created the Taliban, which is the root of the problem in Afghanistan. Delhi's view is further formed by the use of Islamist terrorism and extremism by Pakistan's military to attack Indian civilians and undermine India's influence in the region. India would prefer that Western troops stay in Afghanistan, while increasing diplomatic and military ties and other efforts to bolster its relationship with Kabul.[12]

Moscow's relationship with Delhi is, on the surface, a friendly one, but it lacks much real substance beyond Russian military sales to India. India was one of the few countries that refused to condemn the Soviet invasion of Afghanistan in 1979. Russia does not oppose Delhi's increasing political presence in Afghanistan, though the two countries do not collaborate on issues pertaining to the country's future. Moscow is performing a balancing act in its relationships with Beijing and Delhi, trying not to step on either one's toes, but recognizes that in the future, China is likely to become the next superpower. Russia also values the energy relationship with China—something India has not provided so far.

The largest thorn in Russia's side in the region is Pakistan, which provides shelter to terrorist Islamist groups and apparently sheltered Osama bin Laden. Pakistan has the most to gain under the renewed Taliban control. The Pakistani military views Afghanistan as a "strategic rear" against India and therefore is likely to support the Taliban's return to Kabul. The question for Russia is, will there be sufficient control by Islamabad to prevent the Taliban from undermining the Central Asian allies of Moscow? Pakistanis share an ethnic link with Afghanistan because of their large Pashtun populations—an Eastern Iranian ethnic group.[13] Any stable government in Afghanistan will have to involve its Pashtun population, and Pakistan holds much sway in determining Pashtun support in Kabul.

From Russia's viewpoint, Pakistan is the nation that served as waypoint for U.S. policy during the Cold War against the Soviet Union and served as the main base of operations for U.S. support of resistance against Soviet forces in Afghanistan during the 10-year war. Yet, Russia's foreign policy towards the Islamic nuclear state is one of keeping a distance. Russia also maintains friendly relations with Iran. In the mid-1990s, Moscow and Tehran cooperated to put an end to the civil war in Tajikistan, the only post-Soviet conflict in the region that has been resolved.[14] The economic ties between the two countries continue to grow, especially in the energy sector. Russia sees Iran as a partner in curbing drugs. Iran favors a power-sharing structure among Afghanistan's ethnic groups in the aftermath of Western involvement so that its Dari-speaking allies do not lose power to Pashtuns.

Russia's "Near Abroad" Worries.

Russia views Afghanistan's future within the context of a larger Central Asian security-oriented framework. Its greatest fears in the region are Islamization as it relates to Central Asia, and the Caucasus and Russia's Muslim populated areas, and drug trafficking. President Vladimir Putin's vision of a customs-free area, the Eurasian Union, aims to consolidate political, military, and economic power in the former Soviet Union back in the Kremlin.

One of Russia's main tools for influence currently is the military partnerships it develops with Kazakhstan, Kyrgyztan, and Tajikistan. The Ayni and Kant military bases, in Tajikistan and Kyrgyzstan respectively, and the Collective Security Treaty Organization (CSTO) are a large part of this. The Kant Air Base in Kyrgyzstan has little military value and serves to "flatter the vanity of Russian generals," according to Kyrgyzstan's President Almazbek Atambayev.[15] The airbase serves as a hollow motion by Moscow to strengthen military ties between the two countries.

The CSTO is a security cooperation pact signed in 2002 by the Presidents of Russia and the former Soviet republics of Armenia, Belarus, Kazakhstan, Kyrgyzstan, and Tajikistan. It seeks to prevent conflict between the nations involved and stem bloodshed from within. Its first test came in 2010 with the ousting of Kyrgyzstan's President Kurmanbek Bakiyev. Russia used restraint and did nothing, which was followed by harsh criticism from Belarusian President Alexander Lukashenko, who no doubt feared the same outcome in his future.[16]

The regimes in Uzbekistan and Turkmenistan are by no means Moscow's allies, but their authoritarian nature and distrust of the West serve Moscow's interests. Bishkek has leaned slightly more towards the West than Tashkent and Ashgabat but still remains a firmly pro-Russian government. On the other hand, Tajikistan criticizes Moscow, and Kazakhstan aims to keep its political independence while maneuvering between Moscow, Beijing, and Washington. What Moscow fears most is an end to the "axis of convenience" it currently maintains. [17]

Russia's greatest fear is a destabilization of the region in an "Arab Spring" fashion that leads to an uncertain political future in each nation. Currently, all Central Asian nations have security strategies that involve Moscow's participation, which suits the Kremlin just fine. In the event of calamity, Russia might also depend on China for support, which has never hidden its approval of Russian military domination in the area, while it continues to grow its considerable economic leverage in the region.

Russia's other serious problem of drug trafficking comes from Afghanistan, mostly from its Central Asian neighbors of Kyrgyztan, Tajikistan, and Uzbekistan. The narco-terror problems plaguing these nations are aggravated by their corrupt law enforcement and secret services and the lack of ability to work with Western security forces to stem the drug flow. Russia will not be able to solve its heroin addiction without a serious commitment from these nations, from Afghanistan, and from NATO countries.

Russia also has its economic power as a tool for influence in the region. The launch of the Eurasian Economic Space and the Eurasian Union between Belarus, Russia, and Kazakhstan, in Putin's mind, will be the beginning of a consolidation of power in Russia's "sphere of privileged interests." As he once again assumes the presidency, Putin will no doubt use his power to push this foreign policy agenda and attempt to horde Central Asian natives into his reunification project. Yet, with the exception of Kyrgyzstan, there are few takers to go "back to the USSR." National elites prefer ministerial portfolios and ambassadorial tuxedos to aisles of Moscow-nominated bureaucrats. The Russian elites, too, are hardly ready to return to the imperial mode, sharing their perks with their Central Asian "comrades."

China and the European Union (EU) have overtaken Russia as Central Asia's largest trading partners, surpassing Russia's economic influence in the region. Russia, however, maintains a reserve of soft power through the control of TV, other media, education, and the Russian language, which still remains a *lingua franca*. Moscow also holds in its grip the hydrocarbon economy in the region. Moscow will use both of these tools to expand the Eurasian Union in order to solidify its hold on the region, push out the growing U.S. influence, and attempt to stabilize its shaky regimes before the Taliban completes its takeover. Yet, time is working against Moscow, as the new generation of Central Asian leaders no longer see their relationship with Russia as the only game in town.

A Central Asian Perspective.

Each country in Central Asia has its own view of Afghanistan and its own goals post-U.S. withdrawal. Kyrgyzstan and Tajikistan are largely failed states. Their governments are extremely volatile, and Moscow weighs in heavily on their actions.

The Manas Air Base, located in Kyrgyzstan, has been a point of contention in the region since it opened its doors in late 2001. Manas has served as a base of support for ongoing U.S. military operations in Afghanistan and is the only base of its kind that U.S. forces have in Central Asia. In 2009, Kyrgyz officials threatened to shut down the base due to pressure from Moscow. The message was clear: a permanent U.S. military presence in the region is not welcome. The issue was resolved when the Pentagon agreed to pay higher rents for the base's use, which now amount to $60 million annually.[18]

More recently, a top Kyrgyz defense official made clear the U.S. military should have "no military mission" at Manas after 2014. The U.S. lease expires in July 2014, after which Kyrgyzstan's government will seek to close it down for military use.[19] Some Kyrgyzstani officials do seem to understand the dangers that a complete U.S. military withdrawal will have for their government. In April 2012, Kyrgyzstan asked the United States to leave its drones after the NATO withdrawal of troops from Afghanistan.[20] Washington appears ready to consider this request in the event of future cooperation from Kyrgyzstan following U.S. withdrawal.

In the expectation of U.S. withdrawal, Tajikistan is strengthening its ties with Pakistan. In March 2012, Pakistan's President Asif Ali Zardari imparted that he thought it was important for Pakistan to develop closer defense, security, and intelligence ties. He floated a proposal that the two countries' interior ministers should meet more often for that purpose, and the proposal was readily accepted by Tajikistan's President Emomali Rahmon at a meeting between the two leaders.[21]

In his address to parliament in April 2012, Rahmon spoke of the dangers of leaving Afghanistan in a situation where the progress made is not irreversible. He emphasized the regional instability that a premature NATO withdrawal is likely to bring to the region and the increased responsibility that Tajikistan will have in the region as a result. Tajikistan has a 1,300-kilometer-long border with Afghanistan that Rahmon called a "buffer zone" in the path of illegal drug traffickers from Afghanistan.[22] Rahmon's biggest worry is that Taliban rule in Afghanistan will increase in instability due to a further Islamization and an increased drug trade in the region, leading to his own illegitimate government's downfall.

Uzbekistan's authoritarian President Islam Karimov is in his mid-70s and not getting any younger. Large changes in Uzbekistan's government are likely to occur in the future. Karimov's regime is frequently cited as one of the most repressive in the world. It is one of only nine countries that received the lowest score possible in Freedom House's *Freedom in the World 2012* report.[23] Karimov's regime is yet another Central Asian government that has much to fear from increased instability in the region, as it is impossible to gauge its support by the military and security services.

Uzbekistan recently gained strategic importance to the United States as a key hub of the NDN during

U.S. withdrawal. The relationship is mutually benefi-
cial, and the Uzbek government is earning considerable sums from NATO passage through its territory.
Karimov attempted to use this position to gain a one-
to-one meeting with President Barack Obama at the
May 2012 NATO summit in Chicago, Illinois, but was
refused by the administration.[24] After the U.S. withdrawal, Uzbekistan will have to take far more responsibility for its own security.

Turkmenistan is more insulated from the problems in Afghanistan than other Central Asian countries but has concerns of its own. In December 2010, a
deal was struck to build a pipeline from Turkmenistan
through Afghanistan to deliver gas to Pakistan and
India (known as the TAPI project for the first letter
of each of the four countries).[25] The United States has
encouraged the project as an alternative to a proposed
Iranian pipeline to India and Pakistan. Progress has
been extraordinarily slow on the project. Turkmenistan stated that it intended to sign a natural gas sales
agreement with the TAPI project member states in
May 2012, moving it one step closer to a real commitment to the project.[26] An unstable Afghanistan would
be devastating to this project. Security concerns could
make the pipeline completely unfeasible, and it is uncertain what a Taliban-ruled Afghanistan would do to
the project.

Kazakhstan's concerns with U.S. military withdrawal from Afghanistan are aligned with that of its
neighbors. Its leadership also fears the spread of Islamic extremism from a Taliban-controlled Afghanistan
and a further increase in the narcotics trade emanating
from there. The oil rich country is the most economi-
cally successful out of the former Soviet Central Asian
states and the most stable state in the region. It is now

a part of Putin's Eurasian Union, though its leadership has emphasized sovereignty in making political decisions. To Kazakhstan, the problems coming from Afghanistan will be a strategic, long-term danger, albeit not an existenital threat.

CONCLUSION

Much is at stake during and after U.S. and NATO forces withdraw from Afghanistan. Beyond the understandable concerns about Afghanistan turning into a base for international terrorism and hosting al-Qaeda training camps, one needs to ask questions about regional stability. The strategically important heart of Eurasia is a region that has millennia-old ties to Afghanistan and was negatively affected by the Soviet invasion of the last century, the mujahedeen/Taliban conflict, and the Taliban rule. It benefited from American presence in Afghanistan and may suffer if a civil war erupts or the Taliban rule is restored post-U.S./NATO evacuation.

Russia is casting an uneasy eye toward Kabul and Central Asia. It is likely that the Russian leadership will blame the United States for any future negative developments in Afghanistan, as well as the increase in extremism, radicalism, and instability in Central Eurasia. Barring unexpected, if not miraculous, developments, the Taliban is likely to increase its footprint in Afghanistan, with chances of conflict by mid-decade between this largely Pashtun Islamist movement and ethnic Tajiks, Uzbeks, and Hazara higher than ever. Only by building a coherent multilateral and multilayered policy can the corrosive influence of the Taliban in Central Asia be stopped. If the United States is not going to build political-military ties with Central Asia countries and maintain consultations with China and Russia, at best case, it will become irrelevant to the future of Eurasia, and in the worst, it will witness Central Asia transitioning to the radical Islamist orbit.

ENDNOTES - CHAPTER 2

1. Dmitri Trenin and Alexei Malashenko, "Afghanistan: A View from Moscow," *Carnegieendowment.org*, Washington, DC: Carnegie Endowment For International Peace, April 2010, available from *www.carnegieendowment.org/files/trenin_afghan_final.pdf*.

2. *Ibid.*

3. Japhet Weeks, "Russia's Afghan Addiction," *GlobalPost*, July 25, 2011, available from *www.globalpost.com/dispatch/news/ regions/europe/russia/110725/russia-afghanistan-heroin-addiction*.

4. Trenin and Malashenko.

5. Lada Korotun, "Russia, US to Jointly Grapple with Afghan Drug Trafficking," *Voice of Russia*, April 19, 2012, available from *english.ruvr.ru/2012_04_19/72295434/*.

6. "Russia Concerned over US Plans to Keep Afghan Bases," *NY Daily News*, April 20, 2012, available from *india.nydailynews. com/business/db4a1fcbaa972fb2d19f339542f996c2/russia-concerned- over-us-plans-to-keep-afghan-bases*.

7. Trenin and Malashenko.

8. "Russia Willing To Restore Soviet Legacy in Afghanistan," *Pravda*, February 1, 2010, available from *english.pravda.ru/russia/ politics/01-02-2010/111963-russia_afghanistan-0/*.

9. Marlene Larualle, "Russia's Strategies in Afghanistan and Their Consequences for NATO," Rome, Italy: NATO Defense College, November 2011, p. 3, available from *www.ndc.nato.int/ research/series.php?icode=1*.

10. *Ibid.*

11. "Russia Concerned over US Plans to Keep Afghan Bases," *New York Daily News,* April 20, 2012, available from *india.nydailynews.com/business/db4a1fcbaa972fb2d19f339542f996c2/russia-concerned-over-us-plans-to-keep-afghan-bases.*

12. Trenin and Malashenko.

13. Jayshree Bajoria, "The Troubled Afghan-Pakistani Border," New York: Council on Foreign Relations, March 20, 2009, available from *www.cfr.org/pakistan/troubled-afghan-pakistani-border/p14905.*

14. Trenin and Malashenko.

15. "Russia Pledges to Repay Debt for Kyrgyz Base," *RIA Novosti,* February 27, 2012, available from *en.rian.ru/world/20120227/171562251.html.*

16. Andrei Makhovsky, "Belarus Leader Raps Russia, May Snub Security Summit," *Thomson Reuters,* April 25, 2010, available from *www.reuters.com/article/2010/04/25/us-belarus-russia-idUSTRE63O0PT20100425.*

17. Larualle.

18. Elisabeth Bumiller, "Kyrgyzstan Wants Military Role to End at U.S. Base," *The New York Times,* March 13, 2012, available from *www.nytimes.com/2012/03/14/world/asia/panetta-meets-with-military-officials-in-kyrgyzstan.html.*

19. *Ibid.*

20. "Kyrgyzstan Asks US to Leave Drones after NATO Withdrawal from Afghanistan," *Trend,* April 4, 2012, available from *en.trend.az/regions/casia/kyrgyzstan/2010259.html.*

21. "Zardari Wants Closer Ties With Tajikistan," *Daily Times,* March 25, 2012, *www.dailytimes.com.pk/default.asp?page=2012%5C03%5C25%5Cstory_25-3-2012_pg7_1.*

22. "Tajik President Concerned About Security After Afghanistan Troop Withdrawal," *RadioFreeEurope/RadioLiberty,* April

20, 2012, available from *www.rferl.org/content/tajik_president_concerned_over_afghan_security/24554695.html*.

23. "Freedom in the World 2012," *Freedom House*, 2012, available from *www.freedomhouse.org/report/freedom-world/freedom-world-2012*.

24. Deirdre Tynan, "Uzbekistan: Will Karimov Get Blown Off in Windy City?" *EurasiaNet.org*, May 2, 2012, available from *www.eurasianet.org/node/65347*.

25. "Turkmen Natural Gas Pipeline Tapi to Cross Afghanistan," *BBC News*, December 11, 2010, available from *www.bbc.co.uk/news/world-south-asia-11977744*.

26. Associated Press, "Turkmenistan Plans Natural Gas Sale Deal with Afghanistan, India, Pakistan Later This Month," *Washington Post*, May 4, 2012.

CHAPTER 3

COLLUSIVE STATUS-SEEKING:
THE SINO-RUSSIAN RELATIONSHIP

Geir Flikke

INTRODUCTION

Since 1996, China and Russia have increasingly come to view each other as strategic partners in a multipolar world.[1] The most visible manifestation of the improved bilateral relationship was the Shanghai Cooperation Organization (SCO), which convened for the first time in 2001. The organization was initially dedicated to fighting terrorism and separatism and flagged the state sovereignty of its members as an absolute norm in regional and global politics. By 2005, the SCO emerged with a more distinct message, claiming to be a complex organization capable of challenging U.S. global primacy.[2] At this juncture, China and Russia issued a joint communiqué, declaring each other as permanent and long-term strategic partners in global affairs. To seal this, they also developed a distinct message against U.S. dominance in international affairs.[3] That same year, China and Russia conducted a large-scale military exercise simulating a collective response to a separatist scenario and conducted under a "UN [United Nations] mandate."[4] The SCO also established a contact group for Afghanistan, seeking a security role for the SCO in anticipation of a North Atlantic Treaty Organization (NATO) drawdown from the region.[5]

While the Sino-Russian relationship has been a capstone of the SCO since 2002, the Chinese-Russian relationship has gone from a declared strategic partnership to becoming increasingly problematic since 2006. In 2008, Russia targeted China as a major export destination for oil through the East Siberia-Pacific Oil (ESPO) pipeline. This "deal of the century" signaled that Russia was the weaker part: Russia needed Chinese capital to renationalize formerly privatized oil companies and replace the costly and insecure export of crude oil to China along the railroad network.[6] To be sure, the ESPO is part and parcel of the strategic energy partnership flagged by Vladimir Putin in 2003, which should bring Russia's exports to Asia from 3 percent to 30 percent by 2020.[7] Still, Russia has been in disputes over oil prices since 2009, and the planned Altai gas pipeline to China has been delayed since 2006, with no pricing mechanism yet decided.[8] Hence, the strategic "energy partnership" flagged by both in 2008 seemed increasingly problematic in 2009-11. Moreover, while China still remains a significant buyer of Russian arms, the period from 2006 to 2010 saw a steep decline in the export of Russian arms to China, as well as increasing animosities in Russia that China may reproduce arms technology and resell this on markets where Russia will be a competitor.[9] Finally, in economic terms, Russia remains the underdog. China has the highest gross domestic product (GDP) in the world; in 2010, it was five times the size of Russia's raw material-based GDP.[10] Hence, Russia is apprehensive about reach of Chinese sovereign welfare funds, especially in Central Asia.

Surely, if China and Russia were to bind together as strategic partners, this would be a substantial challenge to U.S. primacy. As Stephen Blank suggested in 2010, the United States has, since the mid-1990s, pursued a strategy of denying Russia the status of a regional hegemonic power to ensure that no single power — or constellation of powers — should dictate energy and economic development in Eurasia.[11] At present, the Sino-Russian relationship may appear to be a distinct challenge to that policy, among other things through their collusion on global governance, the premise of nonintervention, and their visions of a rising multipolar order where powerful sovereign autarchies can set the political agenda. Moreover, as observed by Jacob Kipp in his recent essay on Chinese-Russian collusion in the Security Council vote on Syria:

> the emergence of a close alliance between the Russian Federation and the Peoples' Republic of China would mean a fundamental shift in the strategic balance of power, not seen since the collapse of the Soviet Union or the American opening to China.[12]

Clearly, both China and Russia are anticipating a tidal change in international affairs. As I wrote with a colleague in 2011, Russia and China are preparing a script through which politics reshape geopolitics; i.e., that "politics" is put before "geo" and that both China and Russia "speak" the changes they want to see emerge and act upon them.[13]

This chapter offers a fresh discussion of factors of convergence and divergence in Sino-Russian relations. It argues that they are both **status-seekers** regionally and globally, and the hypothesis is that while Chinese and Russian interests are **converging** in their common pursuit of status in global affairs, their regional interests have so far been **diverging** in terms of regional economic pursuits and energy. It will start by discussing elements of convergence in the context of the SCO and then move on to discuss factors of divergence in bilateral and regional affairs. Finally, the chapter will conclude on a discussion of Russia's Far Eastern dilemmas, offer a discussion of the Kremlin's moves up towards Putin's inauguration, and suggest how this may influence the Chinese-Russian relationship.

SHORT ON THEORETICAL APPROACHES

The SCO—and with it, Chinese-Russian relations—have been analyzed as a revelation of new multilateral trends, as well as in a realist perspective. For the former, the SCO appears as a power-sharing mechanism; for the latter, Chinese-Russian cooperation within it constitutes a great power constellation that reins in small states and bars out competing great powers.

The neo-liberal perspective would be more prone to view SCO "multilateralism" as a new form of shared sovereignty among states and not solely as a balancing act against unipolarity.[14] Hence, a Stockholm International Peace Research Institute (SIPRI) report from 2007 referred to the organization as a multifunctional organization harboring the "deeper goals" to "include managing potential Sino-Russian tensions or competition," and with the aim of adopting "overt activities [that] are directed first at transnational threats and, additionally, at economic and infrastructure cooperation." Moreover, they also hold that an analysis of the SCO would provide material:

> for the debate on how far the multilateral interstate mode of cooperation meets or cannot meet the needs of modern-day multidimensional security.[15]

A Clingendal report, also from 2007, concluded in a similar fashion, arguing that the Organization for Security and Cooperation in Europe (OSCE) and the SCO could, as multilateral organizations, find a common denominator, primarily because:

> both organizations are active players in international security and are thus likely to have a similar interest in advancing the international rule of law and stability.[16]

The competing perspective of "offensive realism" offers different conclusions and perhaps more viable ones.[17] In this analysis, the organization's balancing capacity against U.S. power would be the central point: Chinese and Russian collusion offers substantial challenges to the world order. Their joint endeavors challenge the unipolar moment of universal liberalism (if there ever was one such moment) and see Russia and China as potential rivals in regional affairs.

Some disagreements are visible as to labeling the constellation as a "balancing act" against unipolarity. First, some hold that there are no prospects for Chinese-Russian counterbalancing since it is too costly. In this perspective, the SCO is held to be the potentially "strongest case for the argument of balance-of-threat constraints."[18] At this point, realist theories find no strong arguments for assuming that Chinese-Russian relations are solid enough, and subsequently, their balancing act is considered one of "soft power." Second, others predict that Eurasia is and will be a playing field where "every side in this multilateral 'game' constantly reacts to the moves of all the other players."[19] In this Hobbesian world, states would be prone not to pool resources, and they would see all multilateral arenas as "stage managing" and platforms for cultivating primarily bilateral contacts to improve their economic and security gains. Collective and cooperative security would be hostage to relative material gains, and "the players utilize all available instruments of power in pursuit of multidimensional ends" and not the "multidimensional security" outlined by liberalists.[20] Under such circumstances, some conclude, they might form balancing coalitions acting out of self-interest, however, and these coalitions may have an effect on the distribution of power in international affairs.[21] This also implies that the mutual animosities between the major players — and their strategic cultures — will prevent them from forging **enduring** coalitions against an outside power.

In this chapter, I apply a third perspective that draws on the emerging literature on status in international affairs. This literature suggests that states that seek to advance in the international hierarchy employ various strategies to reinvent and reframe their foreign and security policy interests with the ultimate aim of reducing the attraction of the West. Brand marks like "multipolarity," a "changing world order," "shifting power dimensions," and "new security alternatives" used by status-seekers would, in this perspective, not be expressions of wishful thinking or realities but ways through which to lift state authority and status in the international system. The underlying assumption is that in regional theaters where they have no reason to doubt their own status, they may employ a strategy of "choosing their own pond" — i.e., to forge hierarchies that boost their position and contribute to enhancing their status in the hierarchy or to make their claims to status more manifest.

Here, a preliminary conclusion would be that status-seekers Russia and China have chosen a pond of considerable strategic energy resources — Eurasia — to push each other upward in the ranking system of states and to create an alternative to the unipolar order. In this context, the order pursued by the two is a realist one — i.e., one that is no less prone to let states engage in realist politics and harness power ambitions than what they supposedly are opposing at the global level. Factors determining their joint status-seeking would then be the scope of common economic and political interests, cost-benefit calculations, the degree of their sovereignty pooling, and mutual recognition/apprehension.

The SCO: A Status Club.

On November 7, 2011, the day of the October Revolution, Vladimir Putin announced that an expanding SCO would serve to enhance the organization's status and that the SCO should "become a basic structure of the global economic and political architecture."[22] This statement effectively mirrors the status-seeking dynamics in the SCO, as well as Russia's emerging priorities. China and Russia use the SCO to define and consolidate hierarchies where they can a) recast themselves as significant actors globally, and b) control internal political developments and enhance their soft power and influence.[23] This particular realist version of a "win-win" game would then consist in securing access to Central Asian resources while keeping out external influences. From this platform, they engage in social competition with the West by framing the SCO as a rival security alternative to that of a U.S.-led security system or finding ways to make the arrangement acceptable in institutional arrangements.

There are two primary reasons for considering the SCO as status club. First, the organization claims to have a multidimensional role, and the actors use the organizations to flag all kinds of "globalized" aspirations, ranging from attracting new members, redefining the institutional underpinnings of the world economy, shifting the power of international financing mechanisms to fit the allegedly new economic power-balance in the world, and pushing for a new world order. Russia has been especially prone to adopt a language of alleged global governance innovation, arguing with President Dmitri Medvedev's lofty assertion at the SCO summit in Yekaterinburg that the "SCO should become a universal arena for solving various questions."[24]

Second, the SCO defines a hierarchy of its own, with the Central Asian states henceforth being accommodated politically and socially in a manner that suits their own interpretation of status. As observed by Stephen Aris, the "special nature" of Central Asian regimes is that "the survival of the state is inseparable from the survival of their regime, as without this focal point they believe the state will implode."[25] Hence, by accommodating Central Asian state leaders in a way that dovetails with their idea of status, China and Russia frame the club's members as out of reach for democracies with a global reach, and they convert that message to an organizational rationale by framing the organization as being an alternative to a unipolar world order. Moreover, China and Russia support each other's autarchies systematically, as when the Chinese daily *Global Times*, in the wake of the 2011 Russian Duma elections, published a leader who suggested that:

Russians have cast their ballots, and they voted for Russian interests, not Western interests. Democratic reform won't bring us respect from the West.[26]

With status-seekers Russia and China as constituent members, the SCO is not only a "multipurpose" organization, but is also used for multiple purposes, global status-seeking and regional security included. Both China and Russia have increasingly underlined the role of the SCO in providing regional security. Indeed, with NATO set to depart from Afghanistan in 2014, the pressure would be on the SCO to develop a coherent approach to regional security other than the somewhat circumstantial Contact Group on Afghanistan that the SCO has had since 2005.[27]

SCO peace mission exercises may seem designed for these ambitions. The largest of these was held in 2005, involving 9,800 personnel, and in 2007, when all SCO states took part in a joint exercise. The 2010 exercise involved the use of Chinese air strike and refueling capacity on ground targets in Kazakhstan, and in 2012, both China and Russia voiced ambitions to further SCO military cooperation within the framework of an action plan from 2013 to 2015.[28] Moreover, the scenario of the Peace Mission 2012 exercise stipulates the use of Collective Security Treaty Organization (CSTO) fighter planes at the Kant Air Base in Kyrgyzstan and troops from all SCO members, with the sole exception of Uzbekistan. The scenarios are mostly defensive. The Peace Mission 2012 rehearsed blocking terrorist incursions in mountainous regions in the north of Tajikistan, which simulates a possible post-2014 scenario. In sum, this may indicate that "Russia and China wish to project an image of the SCO's growing role following the NATO exit from Afghanistan."[29]

If the SCO should serve as a regional security organization, however, it should move from what Stephen Aris calls sovereignty enhancement to sovereignty pooling.[30] This seems out of reach for proper analysis; at the general level, there is a substantial discrepancy between what the SCO is (bureaucracy) and what it claims to be (security). The SCO has a complex bureaucratic organization with multilevel meetings; the charter suggests a comprehensive structure involving a council of the heads of states, a council of the heads of governments (prime ministers), a council of the ministers of foreign affairs, conferences of ministers and directors of other bodies, a council of national coordinators, a regional antiterrorist structure (RATS), and a secretariat. In 2004, the total budget for the SCO secretariat, consisting of 30 permanent staff was U.S.$2.6 million, and U.S.$3.1 million for the regional RATS center.[31] Moreover, Russia signed the agreement to participate in common anti-terror exercises under SCO auspices in 2008 and ratified this agreement in 2009.[32] In June 2008, President Medvedev also presented a law project for the Duma making it possible to share state secrets with other SCO members.[33]

This does not mean that the states are pooling resources. Russia's resource pooling within the RATS seems overshadowed by a more dynamic effort to secure inter-Commonwealth of Independent States (CIS) cooperation in combating extremism and terrorism.[34] The CSTO members have agreed and coordinated a list of terrorist organizations and seem more prone to pool efforts in times of economic crisis than what is the case with the SCO.[35] Russia seems to hedge by using military capacities in many different settings. To be sure, the interstate agreement ratified by Russia allows for regular anti-terrorism exercises on the territory of the members, the last in 2011 in China, with observers Pakistan, India, and Mongolia present.[36] Russia also officially seeks to take part in these on a regular basis, thereby hedging between India and China.[37] In 2010, Russia took part in the Mirnaya Missia 2010 exercise in the SCO framework, in addition to the CSTO exercise, Concerted Action 2010, and bilateral exercises with Mongolia and India.[38] In sum, Russia does not find exercises within the SCO to be incompatible with numerous bilateral ones, including its on-and-off arrangements with India. In 2010, Russia renewed exercises with India under the Indra-2010, involving 280 mountain soldiers instructing Indian soldiers in anti-terrorism operations.[39] Indeed, former Russian minister of defense Sergei Ivanov harbored the idea of joint Chinese-Russian-Indian exercises, holding the first exercise with India in 2005 to be the stepping stone for a "triangular relationship," which Moscow has pursued since the late 1990s.[40]

The apparent flexibility of exercises seems to be undermined by the absence of a sense of deep and committing cooperation among the SCO members. Overall, there have been three exercises: the Joint Action-2003 in China and Kazakhstan, and the Mirnaya Missia 2007 in Russia, in addition to the 2010 Peace Mission exercise.[41] More so, much like what is assumed in the status-seeking literature, the SCO template is brought into relevance in all available contexts. The latest was the attempted transfer of RATS operations to other regions, such as in Ukraine, where these would allegedly be useful to combat unrest between soccer supporters in Donbass.[42] Also, the so-called SCO cooperation against drug smuggling looks awkward, given the fact that the Russian armed forces had no relevant experience in dealing with narcotics and smuggling until 2010 and no relevant representation in Russian state committees dealing with these issues.[43] Indeed, Russian press media have noted that the SCO exercise Mirnaya Missia 2010 was more modest than earlier exercises, with fewer notables and fewer committed forces.[44]

In sum, security cooperation within the SCO seems hampered by great power reservations against intrusive mechanisms and against the diffusion of power through sovereignty pooling.[45] Uzbekistan has been blocking most SCO exercises (with the exception of the 2007 exercise), and other SCO members, like Tajikistan, have been hedging by using former bases as points of attraction for states in the region and for the United States. Furthermore, Russia uses its regional influence and the CSTO as platforms to limit the hedging behavior of the Central Asian states, and Moscow is deliberately vague on any plans for the SCO in the aftermath of 2014. Responding to a question in 2011 on whether the SCO had military personnel taking part in operations preventing drug trafficking in Afghanistan, Lavrov simply responded that "as mentioned, the most important factors are development of economic cooperation, and humanitarian and cultural cooperation within sports and education," and that "the SCO as an organization would not have such operations as a task."[46]

Earlier examples of SCO crisis management reinforce the impression that the SCO rubber stamps state unilateralism rather than defending norms of nonintervention. This is well-illustrated in the SCO response to the Russo–Georgian war in 2008. In the immediate aftermath of the Russo–Georgian war over South Ossetia and Abkhazia, the SCO was noticeably silent and did not take any stance on the issue of recognizing these two quasi-states. The SCO declaration adopted in August 2008 underlined simply the principle of territorial sovereignty as a norm in international relations, thereby refraining from any specific application of this principle in the Georgian case. Interestingly, this was the exact norm that Russia itself violated, and although Russian diplomats interpreted Chinese reluctance as apprehensions that precedents should not be created for Tibetan and Uighur independence, they were clearly disappointed.[47]

The SCO did support the six principles for conflict regulation promoted by Moscow on August 12, 2008, and Russia employed these as a point of departure for talks with the EU on a so-called "new" European security system, thus illustrating a typical status-seeking move. According to the communiqué, "the SCO greets the adoption of the six principles for conflict resolution in South Ossetia, and supports Russia's active role to promote peace and cooperation in this region."[48] This was important for Moscow since it gave Russia an opportunity to claim the status quo on the recognition of South Ossetia and Abkhazia, while the SCO remained effectively neutral when Russia evicted the OSCE monitoring mission in December 2008 and when Russia vetoed the prolongation of the UN observer mission in the UN Security Council in 2009.

In sum, giving *carte blanche* to Russia's post-OSCE preemptive and revisionist security posture, the SCO did not harbor any normative views that could dampen Russian unilateralism. The declaration was a straightforward recognition of Russia's sphere of interests and its right to intervene on behalf of an unrecognized republic on the territory of a neighboring state. Moreover, in Moscow's rhetorical moves toward the West, the SCO's statement was brought to support the Russian framing of events in the republic. The SCO left Russia to draw the conclusions from the conflict.

Also, the lame reaction of the SCO to the collapse of government in Kyrgyzstan is illustrative. At the 2010 summit, the SCO limited itself to statements about supporting state sovereignty and the territorial integrity of Kyrgyzstan but refrained from taking any stand as to the sources of the conflict.[49] Russia's manipulations in Kyrgyz politics were not criticized by any SCO member, nor did Moscow's attempt to rally support around a CSTO intervention cause much alarm, at least not from China.

What that did cause was alarm among other Central Asian states, especially Kazakhstan—as was also the case in the Russo-Georgian war. Underneath the complacent reactions of the SCO in the aftermath of the Russo-Georgian conflict, one could sense increasing apprehension among Central Asian states, making them de facto more prone to seek the protection of the more benign hegemonic power—China. Although Chinese responses were nothing like the Sino response to the Brezhnev doctrine in 1968 and the border skirmishes in 1969, China was concerned with Russian manifestations of interest in the Caucasus and seemed more focused on applying economic incentives after the conflict.

Herein also lays a calculated shift in Beijing away from increased dependency on Russian energy sources to that of making use of the SCO to further bilateral diplomacy with the Central Asian states. Simultaneously, China also stressed the need for global financial stabilization, using the SCO forum as one of several platforms to voice this. The most visible aspect of this was the numerous assertions that the SCO was a "new global economic forum," and the less visible was Chinese investments in the Central Asian states' energy sectors.

The SCO: a Global "Economic Forum"?

Much like in security and economic affairs, both Russia and China have claimed that the SCO is of increasing global significance. Russia has repeatedly insisted that the SCO should be a voice in the global economy; at the 2009 Yekaterinburg summit, Medvedev pushed for new financial mechanisms for the SCO, including a common funding mechanism for aid and development and a separate investment and development bank. Moreover, at that meeting, Russia also suggested that some "transnational" monetary unit should be introduced within the SCO, suggesting it duplicate the experience of the EU in launching the Euro — to have an SCO equivalent of the "ECU."[50]

The SCO did not make any significant progress on these issues in 2009. The idea of a separate budget line or investment bank for SCO projects was reiterated by Putin in 2010,[51] but as of 2011, Russian Minister of Foreign Affairs Sergey Lavrov could only say that there was "an agreement that the work on setting up a common financial mechanism should be intensified."[52] In April 2012, however, Chinese and Russian counterparts announced the creation of a joint investment fund totaling U.S.$4 billion, with U.S.$1 billion from Russia, China, and unspecified Chinese contributors.[53] This came after a gradual rapprochement between China and Russia starting in October 2011, when Putin launched new targets for the bilateral economic relationship, seeking an increase in bilateral trade to U.S.$100 billion in 2015 and U.S.$200 billion in 2020.[54]

Russian authorities claimed optimistically that in 2012, bilateral trade with China would reach U.S.$90 billion, an increase from U.S.$33 billion in 2006.

Hence, what seemed like a remote idea in 2009 has gained salience in 2012. Rather than pooling resources in 2009, China lobbied the Central Asian states in a back-to-back meeting to offer a U.S.$10 billion loan to Kazakhstan, which resulted in new energy deals between the gas giant and China.[55] Why the Chinese have opted for an SCO investment fund now invites speculations. The return of Putin as president might be a factor, as he is considered the major instigator of the China strategy from 2006 and onward. Notably, in September 2011, President Medvedev moved the SCO to the forefront of presidential affairs by appointing a special presidential representative to the organization, and 4 days afterwards, he effectively resigned the position as presidential candidate to Putin.[56]

If the SCO succeeds in fronting economic growth, this may increase the attractiveness of membership. Certainly, the geographical scope of the SCO is already impressive, but the region it claims to have a voice in is volatile and conflict prone. Traditional state reflexes should presumably also be at work when the constituents discuss new members. Symptomatically, the SCO does not define what is meant by "region" in its charter and has been dragging its feet in letting in new members. Iran, Pakistan, India, and Mongolia have been observers since 2005, but there has been no progress in allowing them membership. In 2006, the SCO leaders entrusted the national coordinators to work out rules for membership,[57] and in 2008, the SCO had assigned "partnership dialogues" to Iran and Pakistan. However, in 2009, amid the impact of the economic recession, there were substantial Russian reservations against transforming the SCO into an inclusive status club.[58] In June 2009, new disagreements opened when China and Russia both opposed a Tajik proposal to admit Iran as a member, while Russia also spoke against membership for Pakistan, partially not to jeopardize relations to India.[59]

The issue was to be decided at the Tashkent summit in 2010. China and Russia stood together on a formula stating that states under UN sanctions could not become members of SCO, thus making a pledge to the supremacy of the UN in international affairs.[60] This may have put some limitations on the SCO's extensive regional ambitions; the SCO made its commitment to the UN more manifest, while curtailing its geographic aspirations. The SCO thus also exposed itself to possible pressure from the UN. Evidently, the SCO could not claim a regional UN mandate with member states that have been held under sanctions from the UN. Moreover, such a clause would be even more complicated in the case that a country was pulled in for the UN Security Council after having attained membership in the SCO. Indeed, in 2011, the UN General Assembly debated sanctions against observer state Sri Lanka for its crimes against the civilian population in the military action against the Liberation Tigers of Tamil Eelam in Sri Lanka.

These limitations notwithstanding, as of 2001, the SCO had developed a broad network of associate states and a clearer framework for membership. The membership rules are vague on irredentist claims, but the conflict clause so far rules out the membership of India and Pakistan, although both China and Russia (under Putin's influence) have moved jointly towards making their SCO membership more acceptable.[61] Certainly, membership for Pakistan and India could be likely if the SCO does *not* claim a role as a security organization but focuses on economic issues. Economic issues seem to accommodate all SCO members, and indeed, Russia's focal point in the St. Petersburg SCO summit in November 2011 was dedicated to economic affairs and, among others, the establishment of a multilateral development bank and a developmental investment program during 2012-16.[62] Moreover, in the back-to-back meeting with China, Putin stressed bilateral trade and prophesized rising bilateral trade between the two dominant powers.[63]

On the other hand, Russia pursued a proactive line in expanding membership, proposing Afghanistan as a candidate member and speaking out for Pakistani membership.[64] China remained reluctant to this and stressed that the SCO should remain focused on economic issues. China, reportedly, "has been careful not to pursue military adventures or initiatives [in Central Asia], but to build its economic strength."[65] This ad hoc policy on Russia's part more than indicates Russia's regional ambitions under Putin and the potential for increased animosities between China and Russia.

In sum, enlarging the SCO is definitely viewed as a way to enhance the status of the organization. Since 2011, Russia has voiced this strongly and has repeated that U.S. membership is not possible, while also lashing out at "the arrogance of certain states."[66] Still, while the SCO works to boost Russia and China as global status-seekers and regional hegemonic powers, there are also elements of stark competition in their relationship, as well as animosity and suspicion. The launch of a new Far Eastern investment fund by Putin in April 2012 may be an indication of both Russia's Asian ambitions and Moscow's sense of losing a foothold in the Far East. In this context, Moscow would be better off not to see the SCO develop into a security organization, but for different reasons than China. Indeed, rebuilding economic unions (like the Customs Union) and collective security organizations (like CSTO) seems to be a priority of greater importance than the SCO.

Chinese-Russian rivalries play out in two arenas: arms exports and energy, especially in the period from 2006 to 2010.

BEYOND STATUS: THE BILATERAL RELATIONSHIP

The simplest model to read Sino-Russian collusion would be that of realism: states maximize profit through maneuvering in a region with no single authority and resort to traditional balance and counterbalance against any dominant hegemonic power (or aspiration to power) in the region. According to Dr. Stephen Blank, there are three major aspects of Indian interests in Central Asia: energy, security, and the regional balance of power.[67] This could easily be applied to both China and Russia. China and Russia are no different in their mutual apprehensions and their regional priorities. Their so-called strategic relationship seems rather a derivative of how their separate interests play out in Central Asia than a cementing force in their relationship. Moreover, the SCO format certainly glosses over the fact that both China and Russia are intrusive powers in Central Asia, and hence, the declared dedication to the principle of "state sovereignty" in international affairs has low credibility.[68]

China has been important as a major recipient of arms exports from Russia and has thus benefitted from the bilateral relationship. As China is an energy-hungry power, Russia could be a perfect match for a strategic alliance. Concerning the first, Russia still lists, with the United States, as the largest arms exporter in the world; with Germany, the United Kingdom (UK), and France added, these five held 76 percent of all arms exports in 2005-09.[69] Contrary to the export of energy, however, Russia is heavily Asia-oriented in its arms export. The Asia and Oceania region accounted for 69 percent of all Russian arms exports in 2005-09,[70] and Russia has been the most important provider of arms to China, especially within submarine technology.[71] In the period from 1992 to 2006, Russia delivered arms for a total value of U.S.$26 billion to China,[72] and in the period from 2005-09, China topped the list of arms importers (9 percent of the total), with India at 7 percent.

Since 2006, Russia's export of arms to China has declined sharply. No new contracts have been signed since then, and in 2009, there was no single large-scale defense contract between China and Russia.[73] The head of the Rosoboronexport claimed that 2010 was a successful year for Russia's arms trade and understated that Russia's arms trade with China had "lost some of its dynamics." In 2009, numerous problems mounted in the Sino-Russian arms trade relationship.[74] China insisted that the cooperation should move over to high technology, a move Russia resists for obvious reasons: Russia is concerned that China copies Russian technology for resale to third countries.[75] Starting in 2010, Russia blocked the sales of engines for the aircraft fighter FS-1 to China, as China has used it to equip the FS-1 and compete with the MiG-29.[76] Moreover, India has risen as the primary strategic partner for Russia in this field. Russia has had a dominant position on the Indian arms market, accounting for 77 percent of all arms procurements in India in the period from 2005-09.[77] According to Russian press data, India took one-third of all arms exports in 2010, estimated to be U.S.$16 billion.[78] This includes aircraft (Su-30MKI and MiG-29K), T-90 tanks, artillery (Smersh), and maritime missiles.[79]

A Stockholm International Peace Research Institute (SIPRI) report lists six factors that impact Chinese-Russian relations in arms' export: (1) the low level of Russian technology, (2) competition from other suppliers, (3) the quality of Russian arms exports, (4) Russian arms transfer relations with India, (5) concerns about the Chinese copying equipment, and (6) the Chinese competition with Russia on the arms market.[80] Moscow has claimed that China made a domestic version of the Su-27SK aircraft and resold this on the world market. For these reasons, the Kremlin has had a keen interest in reducing arms sales to Beijing to avoid meeting Chinese competition elsewhere. This is a recurring problem. In March 2012, Russian media suggested that China and Russia had inched toward signing a new U.S.$4 billion contract on the Su-35 fighter jet.[81] Russia wanted a guarantee against copying to seal the deal, but China seems to have been reluctant to grant this. On April 17, 2012, *RIA Novosti* announced that the deal was put off again since the Chinese did not accept the Russian condition of a legally binding contract on copyrights.[82] Russian industrialists feared that China might choose the same procedure as with the Su-27 — to accept the deal and then buy only a few aircraft to copy these with Chinese technology.[83]

It remains to be seen whether Russia can gloss over these problems. Surely, the Kremlin has focused extensively on target aims for bilateral trade. Starting with Medevedev's announcement in June 2011, to

Putin's claims in October 2011, Russia launched new targets for the bilateral economic relationship, seeking an increase to U.S.$100 billion in 2015 and U.S.$200 billion in 2020.[84] Russian authorities claim optimistically that in 2012, bilateral trade with China would reach U.S.$90 billion, over U.S.$33 billion in 2006. Still, 70 percent of this trade is raw materials, and even if China and Russia formally have matching interests in the sphere of energy export and import, the pattern of interaction between the two globally and regionally indicates that they are rivals.

In global energy security affairs, Moscow harbors no illusions as to China's emerging role as an energy-hungry power. Russian press sources are already reading Chinese foreign policies as mirroring China's energy needs, as when Premier Wen Jiabao visited Saudi Arabia in January 2012 to reassure oil deliveries in case of a larger crisis in deliveries from Iran, and Saudi-Chinese investment in the hydrocarbon sector is seen as a distinct challenge to Russian-initiated formal declarations of Saudi-Russian joint ventures with no substance.[85] More so, even in regional and bilateral affairs, the so-called strategic energy partnership between the two also has clear limitations; China held fifth place among crude oil importers from Russia in 2010, the hype around the deal on the ESPO pipeline notwithstanding.[86] As for gas, this relationship is almost absent, and the two have been in skirmishes over gas prices for at least 6 years.

This energy-related pattern of animosity and uncertainty is especially visible in Central Asia. China has skillfully converted its participation in the SCO to concrete energy deals with Central Asian states, the leading states being Kazakhstan, Turkmenistan, and recently Uzbekistan. The China National Petroleum Corporation (CNPC) controls about 19 percent of the

Kazakh oil production through investments made in the Kazakh AktobeMunaiGaz and in MangistauMunaiGaz.[87] Moreover, CNPC and KazMunaiGaz formed a joint venture (50-50 in shares) to develop the Urikhtau field in Kazakhstan, estimated to contain 40 billion cubic meters (bcm) gas reserves and 8 million tons of liquid hydrocarbons.[88] Oil travels long distances from the Kazakh fields to China and is subsequently expensive, and China has also plowed into the gas sector. In 2011, Chinese and Kazakh authorities signed a deal to construct a 1,305-kilometer-long Kazakhs section of the "C" pipeline that will have an initial capacity for 15 bcm annual gas export to China by 2014. The CNPC, which sponsors construction, has suggested that the pipeline's capacity will rise to 25 bcm by 2015.[89]

The strategic energy relationship between China and Kazakhstan is paralleled by a warming of bilateral trade relations. Evidently, Kazakhstan's high ranking as an easy-to-do-business-with country attracts the Chinese, which is not the case with Russia. At the bilateral level, Kazakh President Nursultan Nazarbayev has boasted that Chinese-Kazakh trade has risen to U.S.$20 billion in 2010. China is Kazakhstan's third most important export market and second most important market for imported goods. Chinese loans to the development of iron and ferrous ores are also substantial; the China Development Bank Corporation loaned U.S.$1.7 billion to the Kazakhstan Eurasian Natural Resource Corporation to be used for such purposes.[90] In 2011, the *Financial Times* thus concluded that "Beijing's reach now expands beyond the energy sector."[91] Agreements on sales of 55,000 tons of uranium to Chinese nuclear power plants (estimated to be U.S.$8 billion) were paralleled by substantial loans to the renewal of energy infrastructure (U.S.$5 billion), prompting *Financial Times* to suggest that "the financial crisis provided China with an opportunity to strengthen its grip on Kazakh oil and expand into the broader economy."

The Chinese export of Special Economic Zones (SEZ) so lavishly practiced in Africa has also made an imprint in Central Asia. As of 2011, there are four SEZ in Kyrgyzstan, nine in Kazakhstan, 10 in Turkmenistan, four in Tajikistan, and one in Uzbekistan, many of which are initiated by the countries themselves to attract international investments.[92] China has boosted Chinese-Kazakh relations by setting up an SEZ as a special entry point for Chinese goods arriving to Kazakhstan, as well as into the Kazakh-Belarus-Russia Custom's Union.[93] At current, Kazakhstan has nine such zones, and the one mentioned is in the Chinese border zone, Yili.[94]

Kazakhstan's President Nursultan Nazarbayev signed a law in 2011 for the further development of these zones.[95] According to this law, the SEZ are exempt from the regulations of the Customs Union, and hence, China should not fear that there are any restrictions imposed on SEZ economic activity from Russia.[96] Indeed, at the bilateral level, Russia has expressed apprehension that goods may be smuggled into the Russian/Customs Union market, while Kazakhstan will use the SEZ to invite Chinese investments and raw material imports, and assemble goods in the SEZ to be sold in the Customs Union—goods that would be labeled "made in Kazakhstan."[97] This is lucrative for China, and clearly the SEZ also meet strategic requirements for China to modernize and renew critical transport infrastructure. Eastern-based companies invested U.S.$3.7 billion in the region in 2011, and railroads and highways are allegedly being upgraded.[98]

As for relations to Uzbekistan, there has also been substantial activity after the 2008-09 financial crises. President Karimov visited China in April 2011 and struck deals on a Chinese U.S.$5 billion investment in the energy and banking sector, as well as an agreement to swap currencies for U.S.$106 million. Karimov also pledged to finish construction of the Turkmen-Uzbek-Kazakhstan gas pipeline by 2014, thereby preparing the grounds for a potential increase of gas exports to China.[99] Indeed, in June 2012, Karimov announced that the companies Uzbekneftegaz and CNPC had entered into a framework agreement stipulating an increase of exports to 10 bcm annually. He also signaled dissatisfaction with Russia's monopoly on transport solutions.[100] Uzbekistan is considered to have considerable reserves, 7.2 trillion cubic meters (tcm) according to one estimate, and also a potential for the extraction of shale gas.[101] This certainly increases the room for Uzbek maneuvering. Uzbekistan can, just as Russia can, draw dividends from the SCO policies of shielding authoritarian states from external influence.

Finally, a major source of the Chinese-Russian gas pricing dispute is Turkmenistan. Since 2006, Turkmenistan has practiced a specific brand of energy balancing—i.e., not a traditional power-balancer game but a game designed to pit bidders up against one another and thus secure relative economic gains and higher standing in the hierarchy of regional and international relations. Estimates of Turkmen gas reserves have reached just less than 20 tcm, making Turkmenistan capable of meeting demands from multiple bidders and holding the third largest world deposits of natural gas, behind only Iran and Qatar.[102] China and Turkmenistan have been declared strategic energy partners since 2009, and late in 2011, Turkmenistan and China agreed on a tripling of gas exports to China, from 17 bcm in 2011 to 60 bcm within a 4-year period. Optimistically, the Turkmen President announced that Turkmenistan would export 40 bcm to China by 2012. Still, China has already surpassed Russia as a major destination for gas, and Russia lags behind Iran as well. Russia received 42 bcm in 2008 but was down to about 10-11 bcm annually as of 2011.[103] Moreover, this also paved the way for a deeper Chinese investment in Turkmen gas infrastructure. In 2009, China extended a U.S.$4 billion loan to Turkmenistan to assist in its infrastructure gas projects.[104] In 2011, China invested an additional U.S.$4.1 billion in infrastructure to the *Yuzhny Iolotan'* gas field and would be well positioned to make further investments in the planned Turkmenistan-Uzbekistan-Kazakhstan-China pipeline.[105] Indeed, as of 2012, the CNPC is the only international company holding an onshore Petroleum Concession Agreement with Turkmen companies.[106]

Unable to find common language with China over the Altai gas pipeline and gas prices, Gazprom has made harsh public statements against the estimation of gas at the *Yuzhny Iolotan'* field, saying that such claims are exaggerated. This has provoked the Turkmens and has probably made the choice in favor of China even more grounded. Clearly, and as suggested earlier, a tighter energy cooperation between Turkmenistan and China makes Russia's ambitions to strike a strategic gas alliance with China seem further afield. Russia cannot offer the prices that China gets from Turkmenistan, and, if Turkmenistan diverts gas away from Russia, Moscow would be forced to find alternative sources of gas to keep up its export to Europe. Moreover, the situation is not alleviated by the price games played by the states. While China can argue that it tries to avert sale of gas from Turkmenistan to European markets in fear of Turkmenistan demanding a similar price from China, the Chinese also know that this is the game that Russia is playing, but with a lower cap price on gas. Indeed, Russia has repeatedly been appealing to the notion of "European gas prices" in disputes with China, an argument that the Chinese do not buy.[107] China continues to argue that gas prices should be linked to the prices of coal—i.e., substantially lower than the prices at the European market.[108]

The strategic partnership is also becoming fractured with regard to oil exports. Since 2011, both Rosneft and Transneft have been hinting that the CNPC might be sued for nonpayment of debts reaching U.S.$250 million over a disagreement about whether China should pay transit fees for oil passing through the last part of the ESPO (the stretch from Skovorodino to Kuzmino). Whether or not this will materialize remains to be seen. Like Gazprom, Rosneft and Transneft would have limited capacity to have any substantial leverage on CNPC, and the CNPC could further punish Russian interests in Central Asia.

True, Russia has alternative ways of exercising leverage on the Central Asian states, and it does so most successfully in Tajikistan and Kyrgyzstan, neither of which has substantial hydrocarbon resources. Here both the Customs Union with Kazakhstan and Belarus, as well as the CSTO, are central. Shortly after launching his reselection, Kyrgyzstan and Tajikistan both "joined" the Customs Union under substantial pressure. Other alternatives were scarce; Gazprom supplies 90 percent of Kyrgyzstan's fuel, and remittances from the Kyrgyz and Tajik labor force in Russia amount to half of these countries' GDP.[109] Any political crisis between Tajikistan and Kyrgyzstan with Russia would also have an impact on labor migrants in Russia.[110] For Russia, Customs Union membership serves clear political purposes; Russia can place border control units along the outer perimeter of the Union, thus regaining access to border controls that have been lost.[111] In Moscow's relationship to Tajikistan, this has been a continuous issue, with Moscow insisting on the return of Russian border guards to the Tajik-Afghan border. Tajikistan has resisted this by expressing preferences for a U.S.-led border solution pledged by the United States in October 2011.[112] Russia has resisted this fiercely, and Putin has launched this partially as a task for the Customs Union (with Belarus and Kazakhstan).[113] Moreover, throughout 2011, Medvedev also insisted that the Russian basing rights (with the 201st Division) should be prolonged for 49 years. Tajikistan responded by demanding a higher rental fee for the base.

Russia has leverage over both, however. Kyrgyzstan consumes about one million tons of fuel annually from Russian refineries, and Russia has imposed harsh taxation on oil products to the country from 2010. The Kyrgyz might have thought that joining the Customs Union, however involuntarily, might dampen Russian assertiveness, but this does not seem to be the case. In March 2012, President Atambayev failed to secure a U.S.$106 million stabilization loan and to get Russian concessions on discount on oil products, and Kyrgyz debt to Russia is mounting.[114] The presence of Russia's some 6,000 troops in Tajikistan also continues to keep Tajikistan in Russia's orbit and within reach for claims that this is a base within the CSTO designed to promote "collective security" in the region.[115]

Russia's hegemonic claims within the recast Eurasian institutional framework might sharpen under

Putin. Evidently, this may also be paralleled by a more posturing Asia strategy to provide for Russian economic interests in the far east.

RUSSIA'S FAR EAST: INCREASING APPREHENSIONS

The returning fear of Russia is not only that China should challenge Russia's traditional hegemony in Central Asia — which it does — but also Russia's Far East territory. The Eastern part of Russia is populated by 6.7 million people, and the electoral result of the 2011 Duma elections were dismal for the whole of the Siberian Federal District.[116] In the 12 federal subjects in this district, the average support for United Russia was down 18.5 percent, with a low -3.92 in Tuva, and a high 25.23 in Novosibirsk Oblast.[117] In the Far Eastern District,[118] United Russia did not fare any better. The average decline of the nine federal subjects here was -18.3 percent. Subsequently, the press made Trenin's "losing Siberia" vision of 2003 a short-lived mantra in the major headlines before it was released by preparatory articles for the presidential election, all on the contributions of the Medvedev-Putin tandem to democracy.[119]

Starting from 2010-11, the Russian government directed attention to established SEZ in the Siberian region. Putin visited the Tomsk SEZ in 2011,[120] boasting that the SEZ, established in 2005, was now a center for 50 resident companies doing high technologies. As for China, it has established three SEZ in Russia — two in Siberia and one in St. Petersburg. The one in St. Petersburg is in real estate, while the Ussuriysk is dedicated to industrial enterprises and investments, and the Tomsk SEZ to forestry. Russian-Chinese SEZ cooperation on forestry dates back to November 2000.[121]

Clearly, states use economic power to gain influence and to secure access to export and import markets, and China is no exception. China uses these SEZ to enhance its soft power (influence by example and attraction), secure access to resources, and project strategic economic power. But among the 19 SEZ adopted, few seem to be centered on resource extraction except the Tomsk SEZ.[122] As mentioned previously, China seems to implement a similar strategy towards Central Asian states as towards Russia — to utilize SEZ as point of entry for Chinese production while using strategic investment tools and soft power to strike lucrative bilateral bargains in the energy sector. This implies direct soft power competition with Russia over Central Asia, a perspective that the Kremlin is waking up to.

Russian authorities seem to vacillate between seeing China as an example and a competitor. In this context, the Chinese model seems attractive for the Kremlin, etc. In Tomsk, Putin seemed inclined to enter into a competition over modernization, stating that:

> we have made some accomplishments over the past few years. By this, I mean special economic zones, the program for establishing technology parks and business think tanks. . . .[123]

His minister for development, Elvira Naibuillina, was more explicit in singling out China as an example:

> In China, such zones are already producing more than half the GDP. This is a very significant share. China set up its first five special economic zones in 1980, that is, 30 years ago, and now they are playing a major role in its economic development.[124]

As of 2011, Russian authorities boasted having 24 SEZ and 13 science cities modeled on the tax exceptions of the Chinese. Spending on science cities was estimated to be a meager 600 million Russian rubles (RUR), while Putin stated that the federal budget allocation to SEZ for 2011 would be 17.5 billion RUR, in addition to an alleged 28.3 billion RUR infrastructure investment already made. Yet, these zones have severe labor shortages, and Russian authorities lament that there are still mobility barriers inside the CIS hampering a staffing of labor force from this fig-leaf commonwealth.

More challenging are demographic and economic developments further east. For Moscow, the viability of the Far East is of primary importance for the territorial integrity of the Russian Federation and for Russia's foothold in the Asia-Pacific region.[125] The Russian Ministry of Foreign Affairs stated in November 2011 that the major economic development will take place in Asia and that the "Asian vector has been moved to the forefront of Russian diplomacy."[126] Symptomatically, in April 2012, weeks before the inauguration, the Kremlin launched a huge Sovereign Wealth Fund-sponsored investment and development project for the Far Eastern regions in Russia. The development company was to be granted mining rights (gold, minerals) and licenses, as well as vital stakes in the energy and natural resource sectors (estimated to U.S.$17 billion). Comparing it to Ivan the Terrible's division of lands into the *zemshchina* and the *oprichina*,[127] news commentators stressed that the development corporation de facto supersedes state-owned hydrocarbon companies, such as Gazprom and Rosneft, and also regional authorities.[128] Evidently, this is a new twist in Putin's centralized regional policy and a structure that side-steps government structures and leaves modernization to be a key priority of a closed network of government officials.

CONCLUSION

This chapter discussed the Chinese-Russian relationship along the axis of status-seeking and regional rivalries. The primary argument has been that although the SCO effectively may enhance both Russia's and China's status in international affairs, and although they may use their status positioning in the UN Security Council to soft-balance against U.S. dominance, their interests do not fully converge at the regional level. In terms of *convergence*, both China and Russia could benefit from a more cooperative relationship in energy export and import, with Russia having flagged an ambition to increase exports eastward, and China expectedly jumping from a demand of 85 bcm natural gas in 2008 to a 395 bcm gas demand in 2035.[129] China also seeks to lessen its dependence on Middle Eastern oil. Being an energy-hungry maritime great power in Asia, China finds the SCO convenient as an arrangement that plows new energy inroads for it in Central Asia while securing its strategic inland backyard. It has been argued that for Russia, the SCO has primarily been (and is) a reentry ticket into Central Asia, where it lost control and prestige in the latter part of the Yeltsin period. The SCO could provide Russia with the status as a pragmatic regional power, able to find new ways in which to address regional issues. The SCO also provided Russia with a diplomatic framework for its regional initiatives in collective CIS security (the CSTO), and finally, a framework for developing economic cooperation and flagging Eastern

Russia as an "energy hub." Finally, the SCO also adds to their soft-balancing capacity. Through this arrangement, both China and Russia have created a notion of an alternative to U.S. influence, while at the same time enveloping the Central Asian states in a regional constellation that cuts them off from setting up a regional constellation consisting of only Central Asian states.

In terms of *divergence*, other factors are at play. As states dedicated to sovereignty, neither Russia nor China is prone to pin security on multilateral arrangements. In this sense, the prospects for a Chinese-Russian counterbalance against U.S. power are clear, and it is limited to various attempts of "soft balancing."[130] How this will spell out regionally depends on China's and Russia's interests and the capacity of the SCO to move from sovereignty enhancement to sovereignty pooling. Indeed, while soft-balancing may have been a proper strategy when the SCO was initiated, it may look different in 2012 and beyond. Two factors may be brought to illustrate this. First, after the impact of the 2008 economic crisis, Russia may have few other options than to return to this partnership with a harder economic and security agenda. The BRIC (Brazil, Russia, India, and China) experiment has brought little to Russia's foreign policy, and the task of modernizing the Russian north and east is looming while the south is becoming an unruly area where Russia cannot seek status effectively — the winter Olympics in 2014 notwithstanding.

Second, the main architect behind Russia's energy power strategy, Putin, may bring the Sino-Russian relationship back into center court simply because Russia is creating a set of strained relations with the West that were brought to the surface in the 2012 presidential "campaign." Given the fact that the SCO is an alliance that excludes U.S. membership (and also observer status), China and Russia could find that their mutual rapprochement could be the only viable strategic choice after 2014, given NATO withdrawal from Afghanistan.[131]

In sum, even if China and Russia might find it strategically convenient to enhance the significance of their mutual relationship once more, it's not certain that they will return with a cordial embrace, nor does it mean that the SCO will act coherently from 2014 and beyond, predictions that it would notwithstanding.[132] With NATO set to leave, both China and Russia may find themselves confronted with regional challenges that could make their promises of building an alternative to U.S. prominence look empty. On the other hand, it could also prepare both for moving beyond what Bobo Lo called the "axis of convenience." True, Lo suggests that world geopolitics:

is not based on fixed and long-lasting strategic partnerships, let alone alliances, but on much more supple arrangements that are frequently opportunistic, noncommittal, and volatile.[133]

But whenever there is a security void, there are also powers that may make claims. There will be such a void when NATO leaves Afghanistan.

ENDNOTES - CHAPTER 3

1. Agreements of confidence-building measures and mutual military reductions along the border were signed already in 1996, and the 1998 and 1999 summits developed rudimentary frames for economic cooperation and fight against terrorism and separatism. See Julie Wilhelmsen and Geir Flikke, "Chinese-Russian Convergence and Central-Asia," *Journal of Geopolitics*, Vol. 16, 2010, pp. 865-901.

2. The 2005 summit declaration flagged the Shanghai Cooperation Organization (SCO) a multilateral effort to fight terrorism and separatism regionally, and China and Russia demanded the United States set a time limit for its presence in Central Asia. The Russian press has regularly referred to this exercise as having taken place under a "Taiwan scenario," thus underlining the distinct challenge to U.S. interests. See "Indiyskiy front rossiyskikh gornykh egerey," *Nezavisimaya gazeta*, October 15, 2010, available from *www.ng.ru/world/2010-10-15/1_india.html*.

3. "Russia - Closer Relations With China," *East Asian Strategic Review*, Tokyo, Japan: National Institute for Defense Studies, 2006, p. 182.

4. *Ibid.*, p. 184. China provided 8,000 of the total 10,000 troops involved in the exercise. See John Berryman, "Russia and China in Eurasia," Maria Raquel Freire and Roger E. Kanet, eds., *Key Players and Regional Dynamics in Eurasia*, Basingstoke, Hampshire, UK: Palgrave Macmillan, 2010, pp. 126-145, especially p. 134.

5. The first Contact Group meeting on Afghanistan was held in Peking in November 2005, and at that juncture, the SCO pledged economic and humanitarian support for Afghanistan. See "Otvet ofitsial'nogo predstavitelya MID . . .," Ministry of Foreign Affairs official site of the Russian Federation, November 8, 2005, available from *www.mid.ru/bdomp/Brp_4.nsf/arh/8481C3A8C850437BC3 2570B3006B0E9F?OpenDocument*.

6. The Russian company Rosneft took a loan from China to buy the rest of the YUKOS company in 2004 and committed itself to a targeted export of oil to China by railroad. East Siberia-Pacific Oil (ESPO) supplanted this export.

7. Alexandros Petersen and Katinka Barysch, *Russia, China, and the Geopolitics of Energy in Central* Asia, London, UK: Centre for European Reform, 2010, p. 6. This aim may seem unreachable unless Moscow succeeds in bringing smaller oil and gas companies in Siberia in on selling hydrocarbons to the proposed pipelines. For these purposes, the Kremlin introduced a new tax code in October 2011. On the other hand, the return of Putin may alter this. In the fall of 2011, Putin claimed that all pricing businesses with China on oil were cleared, and he reiterated the Asian strategy framed by him from 2006 onward.

8. Sergei Blagov, "Russia Claims Settlement of Energy pricing Disputes With China," *Eurasia Daily Monitor*, October 26, 2011.

9. Linda Jakobson *et al.*, "China's Energy and Security relations with Russia," SIPRI Policy Paper No. 29, Stockholm, Sweden: Stockholm International Peace Research Institute, 2011.

10. Berryman, pp. 126-45, especially p. 128.

11. Stephen Blank, "International Rivalries in Eurasia," in Freire and Kanet, eds., *Key Players and Regional Dynamics in Eurasia*, pp. 29-54, especially p. 31.

12. Jacob Kipp, "Possible Sub-Texts to the Sino-Russian Veto of the Security Council Resolution on Syria," *Eurasia Daily Monitor*, February 29, 2012. An alternative view is given by Allen C. Lynch:

> while often frustrated by the West's resistance to his notion of partnership [to partner with the US and the EU and preserve predominance in Eurasia], Putin never entertained illusions that alliances elsewhere, for instance with China, could compensate for the centrality of Russia's dense and complex set of relationships with Western Europe, North America and Japan.

Allen C. Lynch, *Vladimir Putin and Russian Statecraft*, Washington, DC: Potomac Books, 2011, p. 95.

13. Wilhelmsen and Flikke, pp. 865-901, especially p. 866.

14. Stephen Aris, "The Shanghai Cooperation Organisation: 'Tackling the Three Evils.' A Regional Response to Non-Traditional Security Challenges or an Anti-Western Bloc?" *Europe-Asia Studies*, Vol. 61, No. 3, 2009.

15. Alyson J. K. Bailes, Pal Dunay, Pan Guang, and Mikhail Troitsky, "The Shanghai Cooperation Organization," *SIPRI Policy Brief No. 17*, Stockholm, Sweden: Stockholm International Peace Research Institute, 2007, preface, pp. 1-3.

16. Marcel de Haas, "The Shanghai Cooperation Organization and the OSCE: Two of a Kind?" *Helsinki Monitor*, Vol. 18, No. 246, 2007, p. 246.

17. The term 'offensive realism' is used by John Mearsheimer. See John Mearsheimer, *The Tragedy of Great Power Politics*, New York: Norton, 2001.

18. Stephen G. Brooks and William C. Wohlforth, *World Out of Balance: International Relations and the Challenge of American Primacy*, Princeton, NJ, and Oxford, UK: Princeton University Press: 2008, pp. 72-73.

19. Blank, "International Rivalries in Eurasia," pp. 29-54, especially p. 30.

20. *Ibid.*, p. 37.

21. As John Berryman suggests, "pragmatic *realpolitik* imperatives have largely shaped the construction of this new security relationship." See Berryman, pp. 126-145, especially p. 129.

22. Sergei Blagov, "Shanghai Cooperation Organization Considers Expansion," *Eurasia Daily Monitor*, November 29, 2011.

23. See Deborah Welch Larson and Alexei Shevchenko, "Status Seekers: Chinese and Russian Responses to U.S. Primacy," *International Security*, Vol. XXXIV, No. 4, 2010, pp. 72-73.

24. "BRIK za ShOSom," *Rossiyskaya gazeta*, June 18, 2009, available from *www.rg.ru/2009/06/18/shos.html*.

25. Stephen Aris tends to dismiss these readings of the SCO as overlooking its genuine multilateral nature. I find the genuine multilateralism of the SCO less convincing. Aris *op.cit.*

26. "Russian Democracy Receives Little Applause," *Global Times*, December 5, 2011, available from *www.globaltimes.cn/ NEWS/tabid/99/ID/687107/Russian-democracy-receives-little-applause.aspx*.

27. The SCO indicates what it is doing for Afghanistan. Russia's holding of a conference on Afghanistan in 2009 created no clarity as to the future role of the SCO in regional security, however. Russia held a consultation meeting between ministers of foreign affairs in Moscow on January 25, 2010, trying to hammer out a regional approach, but there is limited information about what came out of it. See *www.mid.ru/bdomp/Brp_4.nsf/arh/C4F607C5866 0238AC32576B70043DA4C?OpenDocument*.

28. Roger McDermott, "Beijing-Moscow Axis Drives Preparations for Peace Mission 2012," *Eurasia Daily Monitor*, May 1, 2012.

29. *Ibid.*

30. Aris.

31. Bailes *et al.*, p. 5.

32. "Materialy k zasedaniyu prezidiuma pravitel'stva . . .," The Russian Governmental Web portal June 1, 2009.

33. "Shpionskie igry Dushanbe i Bishkeka," *Nezavisimoe voennoe obozrenie*, September 11, 2009, available from *nvo.ng.ru/spforces/2009-09-11/11_kirgizia.html*.

34. "Krizis obostryayet terroristicheskie ugrozy," *Nezavisimoe voennoe obozrenie*, July 3, 2009, available from *nvo.ng.ru/spforces/2009-07-03/1_terror.html*.

35. "Banditov vzyali na karadash," *Nezavisimoe voennoe obozrenie*, March 20, 2009, available from *nvo.ng.ru/wars/2009-03-20/1_bandits.html*.

36. "Indiyskie voyska priobretayet novy oblik," *Nezavisimoe voennoe obozrenie*, September 9, 2011, available from *nvo.ng.ru/forces/2011-09-09/1_india.html*.

37. Russian experts have held, however, that exercises and joint operations are two different things, and seem to be apprehensive about this. *Ibid.*

38. "Armeyskaya reforma pomogaet boyevoy podgotovke," *Nezavisimoe voennoe obozrenie*, December 10, 2010, available from *nvo.ng.ru/realty/2010-12-10/1_reform.html*. The article also mentioned a renewal of exercises with U.S. forces as an option.

39. "Indiyskiy front rossiyskih gornykh egerey," *Nezavisimaya Gazeta*, October 15, 2010, available from *www.ng.ru/world/2010-10-15/1_india.html*.

40. *Ibid.*, Russian pundits still see no obstacles for such exercises, and argue that it would be a win-win situation for Russia to have India in the SCO and regular tripartite exercises between the three most powerful states in the SCO. Evidently, Russia would rather see this become a reality than having India plowing too deep into the Central Asian states (like China), a region that "New Delhi gives top priority," and about which it is not too public. See Amit Das Gupta, "India and Central Asia," in Freire and Kanet, eds., *Key Players and Regional Dynamics in Eurasia*, pp. 146-163, especially p. 146.

41. "Strany ShOS snova vyidut na voennye ucheniya," *Nezavisimoe voennoe obozrenie*, April 30, 2009, available from *nvo.ng.ru/news/2009-04-30/100_shos.html*.

42. "Antiterror so sportivnym uklonom," *Nezavisimoe voennoe obozrenie*, June 24, 2011, available from *nvo.ng.ru/spforces/2011-06-24/1_antiterror.html*. It certainly remains to be seen whether the recent bomb blasts in the city of Dneporpetrovsk (April 2012) may serve as a pretext for making either the Collective Security Treaty Organization (CSTO) or SCO anti-terror exercises appear as "needed."

43. "Vooruzhennye antigeroinovye sily," *Nezavisimaya Gazeta*, September 27, 2010, available from *www.ng.ru/nvo/2010-09-27/1_antiheroin.html*.

71

44. "V armii: Slovami oborony ne vystroit'," *Nezavisimaya Gazeta*, September 27, 2010, available from *www.ng.ru/week/2010-09-27/8_army.html*. Russia sent 1,000 troops to the 2010 exercise. See "Tysyacha voennykh RF primet uchastie v ucheniyakh ShOS," *Nezavisimnaya Gazeta*, April 6, 2010, available from *www.ng.ru/nvo/news/2010/04/06/1270555613.html*.

45. This point is made explicitly by Jeffrey Mankoff, who sees the continuous tug of war between Russia and China on the utility of the SCO as a clear indicator of its limited significance in regional security. Jeffrey Mankoff, *Russian Foreign Policy: The Return of Great Power Politics*, Lanham, MD: Rowman and Littlefield, 2009, pp. 196-197.

46. "Stenogramma interv'yu. . . .," Russian Ministry of Foreign Affairs' portal, May 14, 2011, available from *www.mid.ru/bdomp/Brp_4.nsf/arh/D7BDF81A60CC75AFC32578900051D87A?OpenDocument*.

47. "Smezhniki podveli," *Kommersant*, August 29, 2008.

48. *Ibid.*

49. "Shanghaiskaya shesterka voshla v polozhenie," *Kommersant*, June 11, 2010, available from *www.kommersant.ru/doc/1385715*.

50. "ShoSovaya terapiya," *Rossiyskaya Gazeta*, June 17, 2009, available from *www.rg.ru/2009/06/17/ekonom-bezop.html*.

51. See "Materialy k zasedaniyu prezidiuma pravitel'stva . . ."

52. "'Stenogramma interv'yu. . . .," available from *www.mid.ru/bdomp/Brp_4.nsf/arh/D7BDF81A60CC75AFC32578900051D87A?OpenDocument*.

53. "Russia-China Investment Fund Seen Up and Running by July," Ros Business Consulting online, April 28, 2012, available from *www.rbcnews.com/free/20120428172441.shtml*.

54. Sergei Blagov, "Russia Seeks Increased Trade with China," *Eurasia Daily Monitor*, March 21, 2012; and Blagov, "Russia Claims Settlement of Energy Pricing Disputes With China."

55. "The Ural Summits: BRIC and the SCO," *Eurasia Daily Monitor*, June 22, 2009.

56. "Naznachen novy spredstaviltel' prezidentsa RF po ShOS," *Kommersant*, September 19, 2011, available from *www.kommersant.ru/news/1776880*.

57. Bailes *et al.*, p. 19.

58. India, Pakistan, and Iran were accorded observer status in 2005. See "Vesennee obostrenie mirovoy diplomatii," *Nezavisimaya Gazeta*, March 2, 2009.

59. "The Ural Summits: BRIC and the SCO"; and "BRIK za ShOSom," *Rossiyskaya Gazeta*, June 18, 2009, available from *www.rg.ru/2009/06/18/shos.html*.

60. "Iran vodyat za ShOS," *Kommersant*, June 10, 2010, available from *www.kommersant.ru/doc/1383916*.

61. Blagov, "Shanghai Cooperation Organization Considers Expansion."

62. "SCO PMs Agree Project Activity Development Plan until 2016," December 5, 2012.

63. *Eurasia Daily Monitor* on economic growth.

64. Rafaello Pantucci, "The Limits of Regional Cooperation in Asia," *Foreign Policy*, November 16, 2011, available from *afpak.foreignpolicy.com/posts/2011/11/16/the_limits_of_regional_cooperation_in_south_asia*.

65. Roman Muzalevski, "India Seeks to Project Power In and Out of Central Asia," *Eurasia Daily Monitor*, October 17, 2011.

66. Vladimir Fedoruk, "Russia, China don't see US in SCO," *The Voice of Russia*, November 1, 2011, available from *english.ruvr.ru/2011/11/01/59706557.html*; and Rafaello Pantucci.

67. Stephen Blank, "How Durable and Sustainable is Indo-American Cooperation in South and Central Asia?" paper presented to the SSI-Dickinson College Conference Cross-Sector

Collaboration to Promote Sustainable Development, Carlisle, PA, March 13, 2013.

68. A tempering argument could be the fact noticed by Bailes *et al.*, that Russia could have been better off by building regional arrangements with the Central Asian states than to bring China in on a multilevel cooperative arrangement. Still, this is not an argument against a realist reading. Russia does not seem to have much choice, as it is a former hegemonic power in Central Asia. China is increasingly an actor that encroaches on Russia's sphere of interests, with new and explorative capital loans and investments in the Commonwealth of Independent States (CIS) region and through its pro-active bilateral energy policies in Central Asia. Bailes *et al.*, p. 13.

69. *SIPRI Yearbook 2010: Armaments, Disarmament and International Security*, London, UK: Oxford University Press, p. 285.

70. *Ibid.*, p. 290.

71. Hong Yi-Lien, "PLA Military Modernization and Sino-Russian Military Cooperation," Mark J. Miller and Bahram M. Rajaee, eds., *National Security Under the Obama Administration*, Basingstoke, Hampshire, UK: Palgrave Macmillan, 2012, p. 107.

72. *Ibid.*, p. 108.

73. Stephen Blank, "Recent Trends in Russo-Chinese Military Relations," *China Brief*, January 22, 2009, available from *www.jamestown.org/programs/chinabrief/single/?tx_ttnews%5Btt_news%5D=34389&tx_ttnews%5BbackPid%5D=459&no_cache=1.*

74. SIPRI 2011, p. 291.

75. *Kommersant*, March 14, 2011.

76. The contract stipulated the sale of 100 engines to China, was signed in 2005, and was worth U.S.$238 million. There was also a framework agreement on delivering 500 engines, and China could potentially buy 1,000, with a contract reaching U.S.$3.75 billion. The Chinese price for the copy was U.S.$10 million against 25 million for the Russian MiG. Apparently, the Russian agency

allowed re-export of the engine to Egypt in 2007, and also to Nigeria, Saudi Arabia, Nigeria, and Algeria. Chinese and Russian arms trade competed for markets in Turkey (anti-aircraft systems) and Thailand. "Rossiyskie aviastroiteli glushat motory kitaiskikh konkurentov," *Kommersant*, July 2010, available from *www.kommersant.ru/doc/1407757*.

77. *SIPRI Yearbook 2010*, p. 291.

78. *Kommersant*, March 14, 2011.

79. *Ibid.*

80. Jakobson *et al.*, "China's Energy and Security relations with Russia," p. 17.

81. "Russia close to Sign Su-35 Fighter Deal With China," *RIA-Novosti*, March 6, 2012.

82. "Russia-China Su-35 fighter talks frozen," *RIA-novosti*, April 17, 2012, available from *www.freerepublic.com/focus/f-news/2873118/posts*.

83. "Russian Industry Wary of Su-35 Sale to China," *Janes Intelligence*, March 21, 2012.

84. Blagov, "Russia Seeks Increased Trade with China; *Eurasia Daily Monitor*, March 21, 2012; and Blagov, "Russia Claims Settlement of Energy Pricing Disputes With China."

85. Petersen and Barysch, p. 13.

86. *Ibid.*

87. *Ibid.*, p. 40. Another estimate suggests 25 percent. See "Kazakhstan Embraces Chinese Investments," *Financial Times*, February 22, 2011.

88. Robert M. Cutler, "Kazakhstan Deepens China Link," *Asia Times*, March 4, 2011.

89. "China, Kazakhstan Sign Accord to Expand Gas Pipeline Network," *Bloomberg*, September 8, 2011.

90. *Ibid.*

91. "Kazakhstan Embraces Chinese Investments."

92. Dena Sholk, "Local SEZs Face Substantial Challenges," Uzbekistan Newswire, March 1, 2012, available from *www.universalnewswires.com/centralasia/uzbekistan/viewstory.aspx?id=11496.*

93. In Africa, China uses these zones as points of entry for Chinese goods and as zones to further investments. China has argued that, in African countries, these zones should be exempt from taxes and labor regulation legislation in exchange for an improved investment climate. See Martyn J. Davies, "Special Economic Zones: China's Developmental Model Comes to Africa," Robert I. Rotberg, ed., *China into Africa: Trade, Aid and Influence,* Washington, DC: Brookings Institution, 2008, pp. 137-153.

94. This zone covers an area of 200 square kilometres and an area in China that is mostly populated by ethnic Kazakhs. Border," September 1, 2010, available from *www.china-briefing.com/news/2010/09/01/new-special-economic-zone-in-yili-near-kazakhstani-border.html.*

95. "Nine Special Economic Zones Function in Kazakhstan," *The European Political Newspaper,* February 5, 2012, available from *www.neurope.eu/article/nine-special-economic-zones-function-kazakhstan.*

96. See Grata Law Firm, "Kazakhstan Has Adopted a New Law on Special Economic Zones," February 9, 2012, available from *www.hg.org/article.asp?id=25051.*

97. Richard Orange, "Kazakhstan: that Customs Union Outpost is Smugglers' Paradise," *Eurasianet.org,* February 7, 2011, available from *www.eurasianet.org/node/62843.*

98. Sholk.

99. *Nezavisimaya* stated that 16 billion cubic meters (bcm) of Uzbek gas of a total production of 60 bcm annually is bought by Gazprom and that 5 bcm is exported to China. See *www.ng.ru/*

cis/2011-04-22/5_karimov.html. Other estimates by that same source suggested that in 2011, Uzbekistan exported 10 bcm and had made a pledge to increase exports to 25 bcm. See *www.ng.ru/ cis/2011-05-17/6_uz.html*.

100. See *www.kommersant.ru/doc/1385399?isSearch=True*.

101. See *www.ng.ru/cis/2011-05-17/6_uz.html*.

102. Vlad Socor, "Timely Development Essential For Bringing Turkmen Gas to Europe," *Eurasia Daily Monitor*, December 1, 2012; and Vlad Socor, "New Turkmen Gas Reserve Estimates Confirm Vast Export Potential," *Eurasia Daily Monitor*, October 20, 2011. The South Yolotan has more gas than the Russian Arctic reserves in Stockman and Western Siberia combined (about 11 trillion cubic meters [tcm]).

103. *Ibid.*

104. Petersen and Barysch, p. 52.

105. "Turkmenskii gaz otvorachivayut ot Evropy," *Kommersant*, November 24 2011, available from *www.kommersant.ru/ doc/1822628?isSearch=True*.

106. Socor, "New Turkmen Gas Reserve Estimates Confirm Vast Export Potential."

107. See *www.kommersant.ru/doc/1853708?isSearch=True*.

108. Petersen and Barysch, p. 18.

109. Erica Marat, "Kyrgyzstan and Tajikistan Forced into Customs Union," *Eurasia Daily Monitor*, October 25, 2011. According to estimates, Tajikistan has about 2 million migrants on Moscow, returning U.S.$2.1 billion to Tajikistan (2010). Erica Marat, "Russia Punishes Tajikistan by Assymmetric Means," *Eurasia Daily Monitor*, November 17, 2011.

110. One case here is the arrest of a Russian pilot in Tajikistan in November 2011. Russia detained several laborers from Tajikistan in response to this. See Marat, "Russia Punishes Tajikistan by Assymmetric Means."

111. Erica Marat, " Putin Attempts to reinvent the Customs Union As a Eurasian Bloc," *Eurasia Daily Monitor*, October 6, 2011.

112. Vladimir Socor, "Tajikistan Prefers American Over Russian Assistance for Border Management," *Eurasia Daily Monitor*, October 25, 2011.

113. "Materialy k zasedaniyu prezidiuma pravitel'stva . . ."

114. Sergei Blagov, "Russia Struggles to Sustain Ties with Kyrgyzstan," *Eurasia Daily Monitor*, March 9, 2012.

115. Vladimir Socor, "Warsaw Pact, CIS Peace-keeping, CSTO Operations: Moscow Develops 'Collective' Intervention Concept," *Eurasia Daily Monitor*, September 16, 2011.

116. Created in May 2000, the Siberian Federal District consists of 12 federal subjects: the Altay, Buryat, Khakassia, and Tuva republics, the Altay, Krasnoyarskii, and Zabaykalski krays, and the Irkutsk, Kemerovo, Novosibirsk, Omsk, and Tomsk oblasts.

117. Based on *Kommersant*, December 12, 2011.

118. Created in May 2000, the Far Eastern Federal District consists of the northernmost part of the Asian continent and covers the terrority of the Russian Far East.

119. See, for instance, *www.kommersant.ru/doc/1866753* and *www.kommersant.ru/doc/1866781*.

120. "Putin to Chair Meeting in Tomsk on Special Economic Zones," March 14, 2011, available from *english.ruvr.ru/2011/03/14/47351117.html*.

121. Deborah Bräutigam and Tang Xiaoyang, "Economic Statecraft in China's New Overseas Specialized Economic Zones," International Food Policy Research Institute (IFPRI), Discussion Paper 01168, Washington, DC: IFPRI, March 2012.

122. Bräutigam and Xiaoyang argue that there is little evidence that China's 19 Special Economic Zones (SEZ) are used for

energy security purposes. However, for Russia's case, there is a correlation between a number of SEZ (three) and significant Chinese investments in the natural resources sector.

123. Speech at the Tomsk SEZ innovation meeting, 2011.

124. *Ibid.*

125. Berryman, pp. 126-145, especially p. 132.

126. "ATR prevrotilsya v lokomotiv razvitiya vsego mira," *Kommersant,* November 29, 2011, available from *www.kommersant. ru/doc/1826725?isSearch=True.*

127. These terms are the dual administration set up after Ivan the Terrible's fake abdication and withdrawal to the Aleksandrovskaia sloboda in 1564. Courted by the Boyars, Ivan the Terrible demanded the creation of a separate realm — the *oprichina* — under which he would have unlimited jurisdiction. This realm was parallelled by the old adminstrative structure of lands (*zemshchinas*). See Geoffrey Hosking, *Russia and the Russians: A History,* Cambridge, MA: Harvard University Press, 2001, pp. 122-123.

128. Anna Arutuniyan, "A Far East 'oprichina'," *Moscow News,* April 23, 2012.

129. Petersen and Barysch, p. 6.

130. The term "soft-balancing" is discussed by Brooks and Wohlforth (2008, p. 72), who hold that "Although officials in Beijing and Moscow may see a welcome bonus in complications for U.S. security policy that emerge from their partnership, analysts should not confuse side effects with important causes." According to these analysts, soft-balancing is thus limited to rhetorical ad hoc constraints aimed at undercutting U.S. prestige and forging temporary alliances of convenience to promote visions of an alternative world order.

131. Although Putin snubbed the coming head of the Chinese Communist Party in January 2012, saying that he could not meet in March due to the "uncertainties of elections" in Russia, Russian-Chinese relations may still be elevated beyond the cur-

rent standoffs on gas prices and up to a level of strategic political importance.

132. Bailes *et al.*, p. 3. They have gone far in labeling the SCO a multipurpose regional security organization and one that is effective but not considered as legitimate.

133. Bobo Lo, *Axis of Convenience: Moscow, Beijing, and the New Geopolitics*, Baltimore, MD: Boookings Institution Press, 2008, p. 6.

CHAPTER 4

CHINA'S MILITARY GOALS, POLICY, DOCTRINE, AND CAPABILITIES IN CENTRAL ASIA

Richard Weitz

China's growing military power has attracted considerable attention, but most of this relates to the ability of the Peoples' Liberation Army Navy (PLAN) to project power against Taiwan or into the South China Sea. Those analysts who focus on China's Landpower are preoccupied with scenarios involving a clash between India and the People's Republic of China (PRC). Such a focus arguably has been warranted, given that PRC policymakers have largely accepted Russian military hegemony in Central Asia and the large North Atlantic Treaty Organization (NATO) military presence in Afghanistan and neighboring regions. But the PRC's growing economic and other interests in Central Asia, combined with Chinese fears that neither the United States nor Russia can guarantee a secure environment there, especially given the ongoing NATO drawdown in Afghanistan and the increased instability in the Arab World, means that one can no longer exclude the possibility that Beijing will direct the Peoples' Liberation Army (PLA) to employ its growing capabilities for military intervention in Central Asia.

The PLA is now focused on developing its military into highly adaptable and fully mechanized units that can be integrated seamlessly with specialized units such as logistics, armor, and support. The PLA Air Force (PLAAF) has begun to shift from a defensive force with very little offensive potential to a force capable of achieving both political and strategic objectives outside of China's borders. A premium is placed on the coordination and integration between air assets, ground units, and strategic missile forces. The PLA has improved its training in all aspects of the armed forces, and these improvements can be seen in the PLA's success in multilateral exercises with its Shanghai Cooperation Organization (SCO) partners. Military forces in the westernmost Xinjiang Military District are both qualitatively and quantitatively greater than any in the countries of greater Central Asia (not including Russia and U.S. forces in Afghanistan).

With this obvious military and economic advantage, China would be able to dominate Greater Central Asia with force. However, Beijing has chosen the route of multilateral defense and economic engagement. This course of action is not a surprise, given that China thus far has been committed to a "peaceful rise." In today's geopolitical climate, there are very few circumstances in which China would engage in armed conflict with any country along its western border. These would include state sponsored terrorism, a failed state contingency, or a threat to China's energy security. In the first two cases, the response would likely be multilateral, with PLA forces being assisted by their SCO counterparts. It would be likely that any multilateral military operation would be led by China and Russia.

PRC officials fear that any instability in Central Asia could spill over into Xinjiang or that Uighur insurgents could use Central Asia as a base of operations to mount cross-border attacks into China. With a growing Islamic revival in Central Asia, a region with weak institutions plagued by chronic instability, and a looming deadline for the U.S. withdrawal from Afghanistan, Beijing's anxiety is increasing. China's foreign policy in Central Asia, therefore, could be considered an extension of its own fears about its internal security. As a result, the possibility exists that China may deem a military intervention in Central Asia necessary for its own defense. China also has growing geopolitical and economic interests in Central Asia that could prove sufficient grounds for intervention someday. China's diplomacy in Central Asia is primarily economic, as it seeks to promote stability through economic development and gain access to critical resources such as gas and oil. A threat to these fundamental interests would certainly cause alarm in Beijing. China also regards any attempt by the West to establish a presence in Central Asia with suspicion, assuming that U.S. military units in the region are part of a Western strategy to "contain" Beijing.[1]

CHINA'S GOALS IN CENTRAL ASIA

China has had ties for centuries with Central Asia, but Russian and Soviet control of the region during the 19th and 20th centuries largely severed most of these contacts. It has only been since the Union of Soviet Socialist Republic's (USSR) demise in 1990 that China has reemerged as a major force in Central Asia. PRC officials have used their growing presence to pursue a variety of strategic, diplomatic, economic, and other goals in the region, whose core members are the newly independent countries of Central Asia— Kazakhstan, Kyrgyzstan, Tajikistan, Turkmenistan, and Uzbekistan. Not wishing to remain vassals of Moscow, the newly independent countries of Central Asia have sought to develop ties with China and other countries besides Russia. They consider the PRC less an alternative great power patron to Russia than a supplementary relationship that could help them moderate Moscow's predominance in the region and promote their economic development. The Chinese leaders have exploited this opportunity, but cautiously, not wishing to antagonize their Russian colleagues with the impression that Beijing is seeking to displace Moscow's predominance in a region of such great importance to Russia's economic and military well-being. The substantial overlap in Chinese and Russian interests in the region has encouraged PRC leaders to adopt a low-key approach toward the region. Although China and Russia often compete for Central Asian energy supplies and commercial opportunities, the two governments share a desire to limit instability and Western influence in the region. They especially fear ethnic separatism in their border territories supported by Islamic fundamentalist movements in Central Asia.

The PRC's primary security goal is to counter separatism, terrorism, and religious extremism in Central Asia since PRC policymakers fear that these "three evil forces" could adversely affect Beijing's control over several Chinese regions seeking greater autonomy. Many of the latter worries concern ethnic separatism in China's volatile Xinjiang Uighur Autonomous Region, a mineral-rich area constituting one-sixth of the PRC. Deadly riots between the local ethnic minority, the Uighurs, and the growing ethnic Han population have occurred periodically during the past few decades, most recently in 2009 and 2011. Massive immigration by Han Chinese into Xinjiang in recent decades has decreased the percentage of Muslim Uighurs in Xinjiang to below 50 percent of the approximately 20 million people living there. Many of its local Muslims, like Tibetan Buddhists, oppose the growing influx of Han Chinese into their traditional homeland, which enjoyed de facto independence before Beijing incorporated its territory into China in 1949.[2] The Uighurs have ethnic and religious links to neighboring Turkic populations in Central Asia.[3]

Beijing has pressed Central Asian governments just as vigorously to crack down on perceived anti-PRC terrorists, but in these cases, they have typically encountered less resistance than in Washington. PRC officials have employed explicit and implicit threats combined with targeted economic and military assistance to induce the Central Asian governments to curb Uighur activism in their countries, deport Uighur political refugees fleeing persecution back to China, and not protest Chinese repression in Xinjiang. The PRC government has relied on diplomatic initiatives and direct security assistance to bolster Central Asian governments against domestic threats and suppress separatist activities by Uighur activists. Furthermore, the PRC has sponsored Chinese students and institutions to support their studying Islam and Central Asian countries partly so that they can understand and counter potential Islamist terrorist threats.[4] The PRC has also supplied Central Asian governments with defense equipment, military training, and intelligence data to assist them in combating terrorist groups. China's multilateral diplomacy has focused on the SCO, which, under Beijing's guidance, is formally devoted to fighting the "three evil forces" of "terrorism, separatism, and extremism." The organization has established a Regional Anti-Terrorism Center in which the member governments share information about possible terrorist threats. The SCO also organizes periodic exercises involving paramilitary and law enforcement agencies to rehearse counterterrorism operations.

Through these various multilateral, bilateral, and unilateral initiatives, the Chinese government has proved largely successful in suppressing potential separatist activities by Uighur activists in Eurasia. Central Asians often sympathize with the Uighurs' separatist aspirations, especially since Uighur activists may have been inspired by the Central Asians' own successful drives for independence, and they share the same Muslim faith. Nevertheless, the Central Asian governments, while allowing Uighurs to practice limited degrees of political activity, do not permit Uighurs to engage in unauthorized activities in China and have deported Uighurs accused of terrorism by Beijing.[5] The governments of Kazakhstan and Kyrgyzstan have deported Uighurs following Chinese requests.[6]

China's growing energy needs represent another force driving its increased interest and involvement in Central Asia. The PRC's booming economy, combined with its declining domestic energy production, has resulted in China's importing an increasingly large percentage of its oil and natural gas. Most of these energy imports come from the Persian Gulf and Africa, but PRC policymakers are eager to diversify the geographic range of their foreign energy suppliers. They recognize that oil deliveries from the Middle East are vulnerable to disruption from terrorism, local military conflicts, and other regional instability that could abruptly curtail energy exports from the Persian Gulf region. Under its Energy Eastward Transportation Program, the Chinese government has been promoting the construction of oil and gas pipelines that would directly transport Central Asian energy resources eastward into China.[7] Unlike PRC's energy imports from Africa and the Persian Gulf, which travel by sea, energy imports from Central Asia and the Caspian region can travel through land-based pipelines to China, obviating Beijing's need to rely on vulnerable sea lanes that are susceptible to disruption by pirates or foreign navies.

Besides securing access to the region's energy resources, Chinese officials also desire to enhance commerce between the PRC's relatively impoverished northwestern regions and their Central Asian neighbors. Increased commerce with Central Asia could help promote the economic development of Xinjiang, Tibet, and other PRC regions that have lagged behind China's vibrant eastern cities, helping to realize Beijing's West Development Strategy.[8] Although the PRC's trade with Central Asia constitutes only a small percentage of China's overall commerce, it represents a greater and more important share for western China due to its geographic location. This consideration applies particularly to Xinjiang.[9] The PRC government is developing new rail, pipeline, and other infrastructure links that would tighten connections between Xinjiang—which is abundant in coal, natural gas, and other valuable minerals—and both Central Asia and the rest of China.[10] More than half of Xinjiang's foreign trade already derives from commerce with Central Asian countries.[11]

Developing Security Ties.

China has signed a series of bilateral agreements with its Central Asian neighbors in such areas as border security and military cooperation. Beijing typically has provided small amounts of military aid to each

Central Asian country. Its quick delivery of communications equipment, tents, and other defense items to Kyrgyzstan during the 1999-2000 incursions by the Islamic Movement of Uzbekistan, an international terrorist organization, into that country highlighted to Central Asian regimes China's value as a regional defense partner.[12] In October 2002, China began participating in several bilateral military exercises with Central Asian governments.[13] PRC border guards have assumed most of the responsibilities for policing the joint China-Tajikistan frontier.[14] Sino-Russian military cooperation is also extensive and has expanded from arms sales since the 1990s to extensive joint military exercises.

The PRC government has complemented these bilateral initiatives by working within the multilateral SCO. By means of the SCO—which, under Beijing's guidance, is formally devoted to fighting the "three evil forces" of "terrorism, separatism, and extremism"—the Chinese government has proved largely successful in suppressing potential separatist activities by East Turkestan activists and other Uighur opposition to Beijing in Central Asia. The SCO has established a Regional Anti-Terrorism Center in which the member governments (which include China, Russia, and all the governments of Central Asia except Turkmenistan) share information about possible terrorist threats. The SCO also organizes periodic exercises involving paramilitary and law enforcement agencies to rehearse counterterrorism operations.

The previously isolated PRC defense establishment has undertaken a comprehensive outreach effort in Central Asia, both directly through bilateral programs and multilaterally, especially within the SCO framework. Regular meetings now occur between the defense ministers, armed forces chiefs, general staffs, and border commanders of the PLA and other SCO militaries. Some of these sessions occur within the context of wider meetings among government representatives — such as on the sidelines of bilateral and multilateral summits — whereas others involve only defense leaders. Contacts are even more common among mid-level military officers, especially those of border security and other military units in Chinese locations near SCO territories. Military experts from the PRC and other SCO countries also exchange ideas related to their functional expertise, such as communications, engineering, and mapping.[15] Academic exchanges also constantly occur, with Chinese students studying in the military academies of other SCO countries and vice-versa with, for example, Central Asian students studying in PRC military academies. Still, the best known SCO military activities involving China are the major multilateral military exercises that the organization has been holding every year or two since 2005.

The location of the U.S. airbase at Kyrgyzstan's Manas International Airport only 200 miles from the PRC-Kyrgyzstan border, combined with Washington's long-standing military cooperation with Japan and Taiwan and growing security ties with India, invariably has stimulated Chinese fears of U.S. encirclement and containment. PRC officials endorsed the 2005 SCO leadership declaration calling on coalition forces to establish a timetable for reducing their military presence in Central Asia.

On the other hand, PRC leaders thus far have avoided directly challenging the U.S. (or Russian) military presence in Central Asia. Like Russian policymakers, Chinese leaders are ambivalent about the U.S. military footprint in Central Asia. They see advantages in having the United States heavily involved in suppressing potentially anti-Chinese terrorism in Central Asia. PRC leaders are also uncertain how well China could manage the consequences of a complete and rapid U.S. military disengagement from the region. The precipitous U.S. security withdrawal from Afghanistan in the early 1990s, following the withdrawal of the Soviet occupation forces, created a major security vacuum in the region that disrupted economic and political stability in neighboring countries for at least a decade. Although the PRC's ability to project power into Central Asia is growing, its capacity still lags far behind that of the United States or even Russia.

Developments might lead to the PRC's assuming a more prominent military role in Central Asia. Beijing has given indications that it hopes to increase its military sales to Central Asia. With an increase in defense spending by several Central Asian countries, China may be able to assume a larger role in supplying military equipment to the region. Kyrgyzstan increased its military spending from $44.8 million in 1999 to $79.3 million in 2008. Kazakhstan mimicked this spending increase more dramatically, spending $855 million in 2008, up from $206 million in 1999.[16] This trend may well continue because, as these countries increase their military stockpiles, it encourages their neighbors to do the same.

At some point, China might seek a military base in Central Asia. When popular upheavals led to the collapse of the Kyrgyz government during that country's 2005 Tulip Revolution, Chinese officials contemplated sending combat forces into Kyrgyzstan, perhaps establishing the PRC's first foreign military base. In late May 2005, Foreign Ministry spokesperson Liu Jianchao said China would "seriously consider" deploying troops to southern Kyrgyzstan to help counter "terrorism, separatism, and extremism" there.[17] Local and Russian opposition prevented any PRC military operation in Kyrgyzstan.[18] In late July 2005, Kyrgyzstan's acting deputy prime minister said:

> The deployment of a Chinese military base on the Kyrgyz territory has been discussed at a very high level, but Bishkek will not turn the national territory into a military and political range. We have enough means and forces to protect the sovereignty of Kyrgyzstan.[19]

Sino-Russian defense cooperation is also extensive and has expanded from arms sales since the 1990s to extensive joint exercises. Nevertheless, the PRC has not yet established a permanent military presence in Central Asia. Although the Chinese government was clearly alarmed by the April 2010 chaos in neighboring Kyrgyzstan, which led to the collapse of the regime established in 2005 and its replacement by a coalition government, there were no further suggestions about China sending troops to that country. On April 8, Foreign Ministry spokesperson Jiang Yu simply told reporters that:

> We are deeply concerned over the developments of the situation in Kyrgyzstan and hope to see early restoration of order and stability in the country and that relevant issues can be settled through the legal means.[20]

GROWING CAPABILITIES AND EVOLVING DOCTRINE

For decades, the Chinese have observed the revolution in military affairs (RMA) that occurred during the swift defeat of Iraqi forces in Operation DESERT STORM and the NATO intervention in Kosovo.[21] Chinese military leaders observed that small, well-trained forces equipped with the latest information age technology could decimate much larger forces with great precision and lethality. This was observed while the PRC experienced an unprecedented level of economic growth. This growth has given China the means to revamp the oversized and technologically backward armed forces. The Chinese Communist Party (CCP) understood that in order to maintain its national security in the post-information age RMA world, it would need to change the strategy of the PLAAF, the PLAN, and the PLA. Its oversized military was cut by one million personnel to free up funds for more advanced technology, and it changed from a static and reactive strategy that was inherently defensive to a mobile and proactive defensive strategy that favors offensive capabilities.[22] This transformation has led to a more capable and well-equipped force that uses the doctrine of active defense.

China's military has been in the process of transforming itself from a static, region-based defense force into a rapid reaction force, with the reforms certainly geared toward Taiwan, but also possibly in anticipation of an intervention in Central Asia.[23] In an effort to move away from a regional infantry-based army, the PLA has adopted modular battle group structures like those employed by the U.S. military, with an eye toward supporting high-altitude operations in complex terrains, such as those found in Central Asia.[24] Many PLA brigade and battalion-sized units are now capable of independent operations, offering greater flexibility for Chinese commanders, and China has been loosening its previously rigid military structure to allow for rapid reallocation of forces from one end of the country to another, a capability they displayed during the Stride 2009 exercises.[25] Indeed, one of the primary goals of China's Stride 2009 exercise was to demonstrate that Chinese units could move far from their home region and operate in any environment.[26] The PLA has been focusing on developing what it calls Rapid Reaction Forces and Resolving Emerging Mobile Combat Forces, units that are trained and equipped to move quickly over air, sea, and land to contingencies along the PRC's borders. Chinese special operations forces (SOF) have also been improving in terms of training and capability, and China has established a new airborne division designed for rapid deployment. Such rapid reaction units will eventually comprise 10 to 15 percent of the PLA.[27] The PLAAF has also been ordered to develop a rapid, mobile force, moving from a close air support mission to a more independent combat role.[28]

Historically, the Chinese military has had difficulty sustaining forces along its periphery; examples of this include the Sino-Vietnamese war and the response to the 2008 Sichuan earthquake, which revealed problems with air support. In addition, the PLA is faced with deficiencies in its rapid air transport and high-altitude helicopter support capabilities, both assets that would be crucial for rapid-reaction and counterinsurgency (COIN) operations in Xinjiang and Central Asia. The PLAAF has a severe shortage of long-range heavy air transports and aerial refuelers, precluding the possibility of rapidly moving significant forces to Central Asia by air.[29] This problem has been compounded by China's recent cancellation of an order for 38 Il-76 air transports and Il-78 refueling aircraft after the factory in Uzbekistan was unable to complete delivery.[30] The workhorse of the Chinese transport helicopter fleet, a modified version of the Russian Mi-17, also has a fairly limited capacity in a mountainous environment such as Tajikistan or Kyrgyzstan, being able to carry only 6-8 fully equipped soldiers to an altitude of just 3,000 meters. While the Chinese have developed the AC313 medium-lift helicopter, which is capable of operating at altitudes of 6,000 meters and at temperatures of -40 to +50 degrees Celsius, it is currently tasked for civilian use.[31] Whether it is adapted for the military may be telling of the types of operations that the PLA anticipates conducting in the future.

Problems with air transportation mean that any large-scale movement of units to Central Asia will have to be done over land, likely by rail. Stride 2009, for instance, relied heavily on railroads for long-distance transport.[32] More importantly, in anticipation of the SCO exercise Peace Mission 2010, the Chinese upgraded their rail capacity in the western part of the country and used these networks to transport the military units participating in the exercise, which was held in Kazakhstan. The PLA is closely involved in the planning of rail networks, and over 1,000 railway stations have been outfitted with military transportation facilities. Central Asian analysts have already noted that such rail infrastructure could support a Chinese intervention. The PLA has been actively using rail networks to upgrade the long-range logistical capabilities of its forces—for example, the Qinghai-Tibet railway has been used to enhance the PLAAF's mobilization capabilities in western China. Beijing is in the process of upgrading its rail and air facilities in Tibet and is also involved in the construction of a rail line through Kyrgyzstan, Tajikistan, and Afghanistan, which will be part of the United Nations (UN)-sponsored Trans-Asia railway network.[33] Several railways are also being built in Central Asia to transport natural resources to China.[34] Chinese officials have also underlined the important experience gained by the PLA in long-range rail transport during Peace Mission 2010, including changing trains and switching rail gauges at the border, as well as transporting heavy equipment.[35] Given these developments, it can be concluded with a fair amount of certainty that any Chinese intervention in Central Asia involving regular army units would rely heavily on railways for logistical support, with Chinese infrastructure already having the capacity for such operations.

The 2008 Sichuan earthquake and the 2008 Tibet and 2009 Xinjiang riots also shed some light on China's capability to react to crises on the country's periphery. During the Sichuan crisis, the PLA had primary responsibility for allocating government resources and assigning missions.[36] The PLA, however, had difficulty during search and rescue operations, as it did not have enough helicopters, nor did it have the experience to sustain a high operations tempo with its existing fleet. Noticeable improvement was observed during the Sichuan flooding of 2010, however, when PLA helicopters from various units operated efficiently under a unified command and maintained a very fast operations tempo.[37] The incident suggests that the PLA is making good use of past lessons and quickly adapting. During the Tibet and Xinjiang riots, China's inexperience with COIN was evident, as units had significant difficulties with intelligence and coordination between military and political authorities, as well as between military and paramilitary forces.[38] The People's Armed Police (PAP), employing its counter-insurgency capabilities, was the primary agency used to suppress the riots, although the PLA would take COIN responsibilities if an international intervention was necessary.[39]

The PLA's growing ability to project military power has been most evident in its military exercises in the region. For Beijing, these exercises with Russia and some Central Asian countries, typically within the SCO framework, serve a number of purposes besides enhancing the collective military capacity of the member states. These benefits include improving the proficiency of the PLA, demonstrating new combat skills, learning about other militaries and their capabilities, reassuring the Central Asian members that Beijing respected their security needs, cultivating bilateral contacts with other SCO members, and signaling to outside powers that the SCO region was a zone of special security concern for Beijing.

The first SCO Peace Mission exercise occurred in August 18-25, 2005. Although SCO members sent observers, this event was primarily a Russian-Chinese show. The two armed forces conducted a three-phased operation that began in Vladivostok in the Russian Far East and then moved to China's Shandong Peninsula, where the participants conducted land and amphibious maneuvers.[40] While the Chinese supplied most of the troops (8,000 versus 2,000), the Russians provided the most sophisticated equipment, including Russian Tu-160 and Tu-95 strategic bombers, as well as some 140 warships.[41] The maneuvers practiced during Peace Mission 2005 included neutralizing anti-aircraft defenses, enforcing a maritime blockade, and conducting an amphibious assault and other joint maritime operations. Although their stated purpose was to fight terrorists and restore peace among hypothetical local combatants, the large scale of the air, sea, and ground operations made it appear to Russian and foreign observers like a rehearsal for a joint amphibious invasion of Taiwan, with tactics designed to deter or defeat American military intervention on the island's behalf.[42] The U.S. Department of Defense (DoD) also interpreted the exercise as partly an attempt by China to strengthen its power projection capabilities with respect to Taiwan.[43] The Russian government at least did not seek to impart such an impression. Moscow reportedly rejected an earlier Chinese proposal to conduct the war games in Zhejiang, a Chinese coastal province near Taiwan.[44] Another possible scenario could have been a joint Russian-Chinese military occupation of the Democratic People's Republic of Korea (DPRK) should the regime in Pyongyang collapse. In such an eventuality, other countries might contemplate moving military forces into North Korea to avert a humanitarian disaster (which could include a massive flight of refugees into neighboring Chinese and Russian territories, as well as South Korea) and secure the DPRK's nuclear explosive devices and other weapons before they could fall into the hands of terrorists, criminals, or other rogue regimes. Beijing and Moscow might want to occupy the territory first rather than allow American forces to move so close to their borders.

The more recent SCO exercise most closely resembles Peace Mission 2007, which occurred from August 9-17, 2007. The 2007 drill transpired more clearly within the SCO framework. Unlike in 2005, the armed forces of all six full SCO members participated on this occasion, with almost 6,500 troops and 80 aircraft engaged in the two phases, including 2,000 troops from Russia and 1,600 from China.[45] Peace Mission 2007 began on August 9 in Urumqi, the capital of China's Xinjiang-Uighur Autonomous Area, and ended on August 17, with a live-fire exercise at the Russian military training range near Chelyabinsk, in Russia's Volga-Urals Military District. Unlike Peace Mission 2005, but like Peace Mission 2010, this 2007 exercise, which did not involve military ships, was better oriented toward suppressing a major Islamist insurgency (such as occurred in Chechnya) or popular rebellion (such as occurred at Tiananmen Square in 1989 or Andijan in 2005), presumably in one of the landlocked Central Asian countries.

Peace Mission 2009 took place from July 22-27, 2009. Unlike in 2007, only Russian and Chinese troops participated on this occasion, but, as in 2005, the other SCO members received invitations to send military observers to Peace Mission 2009.[46] The drills began with a single day of political-military consultations among senior Russian and Chinese defense personnel in Khabarovsk, the largest city in the Russian Far East and the headquarters of the Far East Military Command.[47] The two delegations reportedly discussed "the overall anti-terror situation" and "the terrorism trends in member countries of the Shanghai Cooperation Organization" as well as Afghanistan.[48] The operational phases of the exercise took place in northeast China, at the Taonan training base in China's Shenyang Military Area Command.[49] They then spent 3 days jointly planning and organizing for a combined anti-terrorist campaign. The most important exercise segment was a live-fire drill at the base, which occupied 90 minutes on the last day.[50] About 1,300 military personnel from each country participated in some phase of the exercise. The Russian air force contributed about 20 military aircraft to the maneuvers in China, including Su-25 and Su-27 combat jets, Il-76 transport planes, Su-24 bombers, and Mi-8 helicopters.[51] The Chinese military sent about an equal number of combat aircraft, one of which crashed a few days before the exercise began.

The Chinese armed forces contributed artillery, air defense, army aviation, and special forces contingents, as well as logistical support to both sides.[52] Peace Mission 2009 differed from the previous two exercises in the series in certain respects. The operational phase of the drills occurred only on Chinese territory, with the single day of discussions at Khabarovsk looking like a simple attempt to involve Russian territory in some direct capacity. The number of troops participating was much less than in previous years, even if some more sophisticated weaponry was involved in that year's exercise.

In Peace Mission 2010, an SCO exercise that occurred September 9-25 in southern Kazakhstan, the PLA sent a major contingent consisting of a ground force of approximately 1,000 soldiers, an air force combat group, and a logistics group under the command of Ma Xiaotian, PLA deputy chief of the PLA General Staff.[53] The exercise consisted of three phases. The first stage involved consultations among senior political officials and military officers in Almaty. The defense ministers, general staff chiefs, and others involved discussed how to employ SCO troops to resolve emergencies, as well as the global and regional security environment, defense cooperation within the SCO, and other shared interests among the member states. The Chiefs of the General Staffs then issued instructions to start the drills.[54] The next two phases involved combat exercises among the forces that had deployed to the Matybulak Air Base near Gvardeisky in Kazakhstan. Stage two, which began on September 13, focused on joint maneuvers and drills in which the SCO contingents practiced making preparatory fire, mobilizing reserves, besieging residential areas, conducting breakouts, and using suppressing fire at night. During the main hour-long drill on September 15, the forces employed more than 1,000 armed vehicles, artillery pieces, rocket launchers, and other ground equipment as well as more than 50 military aircraft.[55] Phase 3, which started on September 24, saw some live-fire drills, and then ended with a display of combat equipment from the member states, which included some of the equipment that the PLA had displayed on 60th anniversary National Day military parades in Beijing.[56]

The exercise included some 5,000 troops, 300 major combat pieces such as tanks, other sophisticated defense equipment for engineering and communications, and over 50 combat planes and helicopters.[57] Russia, China, and Kazakhstan each sent at least 1,000 troops to the war games, whereas Kyrgyzstan and Tajikistan contributed smaller numbers, though even these represented at least one self-standing operational-tactical group.[58] Russia sent the largest amount of military equipment—some 130 tanks, self-propelled artillery systems, and infantry fighting vehicles, as well as over 100 trucks and about a dozen aircraft from its nearby base in Kant, Kyrgyzstan, including Su-24 *Fencer* tactical bombers, Su-25 *Frogfoot* close-support aircraft, and Mi-8 transport helicopters.[59] The PLA sent some of its most sophisticated indigenous weapons systems, including T-99 tanks, H-6 strategic bombers, and J-10 fighters, as well as aerial tanker and early warning aircraft.[60] The H-6 and the J-10 warplanes participated on their first foreign exercise.[61] With 5,000 troops and considerable advanced military equipment, Peace Mission 2010 was the largest SCO military exercise outside of Russian and Chinese territory. With a duration of 15 days, Peace Mission 2010 was 1 week longer than the previous multinational SCO war games in 2007.

Peace Mission 2010 could enhance the ability of the Russian, Chinese, and perhaps other SCO militaries to work together as a collective security force. Like the previous exercises in the Peace Mission series, the most recent drill could enhance the ability of the Russian, Chinese, and perhaps other SCO armed forces to deter — and if necessary suppress — another popular rebellion (which the SCO governments characterize as a large-scale terrorist movement), such as the ones that occurred in Tiananmen Square in the spring of 1989 and in Andijan, Uzbekistan, in May 2005. The 2010 exercise occurred against the backdrop of continuing ethnic-religious minority unrest in Xinjiang and Tibet, newly resurgent terrorist activity in Tajikistan and Kyrgyzstan, and the deteriorating security situation in Afghanistan and the Russian-controlled territories of the North Caucasus. Hundreds of people had died the previous year in vicious street fighting between Uighurs and Han Chinese in Xinjiang and other parts of China. The authorities, who used the military to suppress the disorders after the police and other internal security forces lost control of the situation, blamed the ethnic rioting on foreign-backed terrorists seeking to create a separate state of East Turkmenistan.

PRC representatives especially emphasized the counterterrorist dimensions of the most recent exercise. Although the member governments most often described Peace Mission 2010 as an anti-terrorist exercise, their representatives and media acknowledged that the capabilities on display could be used to deal with other forms of internal armed conflict as well as a mass terrorist attack.[62] In principle, SCO members might come to one another's defense in case of an external invasion, but the organization's charter does not formally authorize collective defense operations, so all the observations regarding the SCOs having more than half of the world's landmass and a quarter of the world's population are inapposite in that, lacking even a collective command structure like NATO and divided by various competing interests, the SCO members will never fight as an integrated unit. There is also no evident aggressor state eager to attack one of the Central Asian members, while China and Russia—both possessing nuclear weapons as well as powerful conventional forces—are sufficiently powerful to defend themselves without foreign support. In practice, China would prove reluctant to make such a defensive commitment since Beijing has shunned formal military alliances, while the other five governments belong to the Moscow-led Collective Security Treaty Organization (CSTO), whose explicit function is to provide for the mutual defense of its members from external attack.

An important goal is to improve the operational and tactical proficiency of the participating militaries and increase their level of interoperability. Chinese defense representatives have traditionally cited the advantage of using exercises with foreign countries as opportunities to learn new tactics, techniques, and procedures. In this case, they can also use the SCO exercises to practice coordinating large and varied forces with Russia, one of the world's leading military powers. One Chinese writer observed that:

> For China, the drills offer opportunities to showcase the PLA as a defender of peace on an international stage. They help enhance the PLA's military transparency, promote its coordination ability with foreign military forces and improve its competence by learning from the military forces of other countries.[63]

The PLA forces involved in these drills have demonstrated increased proficiency over time, though it is unclear whether this improvement results from the exercises themselves or the strengthening capabilities of both sides' conventional forces in recent years due to other initiatives. The PLA has proved especially apt at using these exercises to enhance its capabilities. For example, the 2007 live-fire drills in Chelyabinsk allowed the Chinese armed forces to practice deploying and supporting a large military force at a considerable distance from mainland China.[64] The same was perhaps even more true in Peace Mission 2010, when the PLA demonstrated improved logistics, command and control, and more sophisticated weapons and tactics. Before the exercise began, the PLA forces undertook extensive pre-deployment theoretical, basic, and combined combat training, optimized for joint counterterrorist training.[65]

In early September, hundreds of PLA soldiers traveled by train at the starting from a PLA training military base at Zhurihe, located in North China's Inner Mongolia Autonomous Region, to Matybulak Air Base in Kazakhstan. The total distance covered during the week-long trip was 5,000 kilometers (km), after which the PLA soldiers immediately began preparing for their drills.[66] One Chinese writer boasted that this represented "a big test for PLA's comprehensive transportation capability."[67] According to Li Zhujun, deputy chief of the exterior liaison of the Chinese command of the military exercises, the PLA moved a total of six contingents of almost 1,000 troops, 1,000 tons of materials, and additional quantities of military equipment. PLA logisticians also had the opportunity to load and unload carriages as they passed from the 2.98-meter gauge used in China to the 2.87-meter gauge employed in Kazakhstan. "By improving the quality of service and logistics in various links," Li declared, "we have created conditions for the soldiers and officers to devote themselves to the exercises in high spirits and full of vitality."[68]

Peace Mission 2010 also involved more demanding live-fire drills than previous SCO exercises. In those cases, the simulated combat operations often appeared as media shows, timed to coincide with the annual SCO heads-of-state summits. In 2010, the live drills occurred over several days, and about 50 percent took place at night.[69] The Chinese Army's helicopters rehearsed their first nighttime shooting exercise.[70] Perhaps the most interesting skill demonstrated by the PLA was how the Air Force conducted its first simulated long-range air strike. Four H-6 bombers and two J-10 fighter jets took off from air bases in Urumqi, China. They then divided into two groups that, following mid-air refueling, each rehearsed bombing ground targets in Kazakhstan, 2,000 km away from their departure base. According to PRC military officials, these planes could have conducted their bombing runs even without refueling.[71] Having the capacity to conduct long-range air strikes and coordinate air-ground battle maneuvers could prove useful for attacking insurgents in Central Asia, as well as combating Indian ground forces further north. A Chinese analyst claimed that the H-6 bombers hit their target every time and that the helicopters were able to fly only 40 meters above the ground in a valley.[72] A Western analyst termed the strikes a "milestone" in the PLA's ability to intervene rapidly in Central Asia.[73]

In order to accomplish these expensive and complex training exercises, the logistical challenges of moving a large force into the host country must be overcome. This is essentially akin to the logistical capabilities needed to project force in the case of conflict. In the case of China's most recent military exercise with the SCO, the PLA used a mix of air and rail transport to rapidly move an expeditionary force of over 1,000 men and their vehicles from eastern China to Kazakhstan, a journey covering 5,000 km.[74] In this same exercise, the PLAAF tested its newly developed integrated air strike capabilities. Four H-6 bombers with two J-10 fighter escorts, supported by tankers and an airborne command aircraft, took off from a base in Xinjiang and struck their targets in Kazakhstan.[75] Successful demonstrations of air power projection are a result of the increased training of PLAAF pilots, who have increased annual training from less than 100 hours to over 200 hours.[76] The PLAAF now trains in all weather conditions as well to give its pilots skills required to field a professional air force with the means to have a strategic impact. The PLAAF has changed from a purely defensive force to one with the ability to commit to a broader — although still limited in comparison to the U.S. Air Force — range of missions outside of PRC territory.

Force projection is inherently linked to the logistical capabilities of a country's military. An army must be able to have constant access to food, munitions, and fuel to maintain combat effectiveness in foreign territory. In the case of China, transportation systems are well developed in the coastal regions of the east, promoting economic growth and allowing for the easy flow of supplies in case of conflict with Taiwan or other maritime neighbors. The western frontier is a different matter altogether; much of the Xinjiang Military District is desert and mountains. To improve logistical capabilities in this western district and throughout all of mainland China, the National Trunk Highway System (NTHS) is being expanded through the Lanzhou and Chengdu military regions, giving PLA group armies the logistical ability to resupply and redeploy as needed. An advanced highway system would give the 47th and 21st Group Armies, the latter of which contains the Lanzhou Military Region's special operations group, expanded capabilities to move men and vehicles to the borders of Central Asian countries. Using the current transportation system, their headquarters in Shaanxi is 3,731 km from the western frontier.

As the NTHS expands over the next decade, the PLA will find that its logistical base has improved dramatically. Because of the need to move military forces to flashpoints along the western frontier, the PLA has created rapid reaction forces and Resolving Emerging Mobile Combat Forces. These forces are capable of being deployed in the event of high intensity but short duration conflicts, conventional large-scale theater wars, and everything in between.[77] The true strength of these new mechanized forces is their small logistic footprint and organizational flexibility, which allows them to fight as independent battle groups in the undeveloped rural areas of Xinjiang and Tibet, while also enabling the integration of logistical and armored units.[78] The unique structure of these forward deployed mechanized units sets them apart from their counterparts in the PLA.

The logistics of China's air projection capabilities are increasingly effective due to the close proximity of PLAAF bases and civilian airports capable of handling military air traffic to the western borders. There is a major PLAAF airbase only a 90 km drive from the city of Kumul, Xinjiang. The Urumqi Airport and Urumqi

South Air Base both have viable launching points for any planes in the PLAAF fleet. Furthermore, they are located within 1,700 km of the capital cities of all countries bordering the Lanzhou Military Region. This location puts the J-11 with a combat range of 2,000 km[79] and Su-30MKK with a combat range of 3,000 km[80] well within effective ranges to support any ground operations in the Greater Central Asian (GCA) region. While this range is greatly increased with the use of tanker aircraft such as the H-6U,[81] joint operation capabilities between ground and air forces, while they do exist, are still limited by limitations in the PLA's command and control capabilities.[82] The PLAAF effectively demonstrated the use of its aerial tanker and command and control planes, as well as the H-6 long-range strategic bomber, in the controlled environment of the Peace Mission 2010 SCO exercise; this bomber has a combat range of 8,060 km.[83]

Furthermore, the PLAAF strategy for aerial combat stresses the targeting of enemy air assets while on the ground, which suggests that the PLA lacks an advantage against more advanced air forces such as those of the United States or Russia.[84] While this lack of confidence to commit to air-to-air combat is unwarranted against China's neighboring Central Asian countries, the PLAAF's preparation for anti-ground operations would make the targeting of airbases a top priority for a first strike in any air campaign. The PLAAF also has a regional air lift capability; its most well equipped heavy air transport currently in the fleet is the Il-76, which can drop 190 paratroopers or three armored vehicles over a distance of 6,100 km.[85]

The future is also promising for PLA air projection capabilities. The Y-9 unveiled in 2005 is the Chinese equivalent to the American C-130J; it boasts a ferry range of 7,800 km and increased lift capacity with the ability to transport armored vehicles, helicopters, cargo containers, or up to 130 paratroopers.[86] The likelihood of airborne infantry and SOF being utilized to attack deep enemy targets in the event of an air campaign is very likely due to their inclusion within the ranks of the PLAAF.[87]

Due to China's landlocked western borders, its short range ballistic missiles and medium range ballistic missiles arsenals can be utilized as a means of power projection in tactical support of ground forces or strategic strikes. The maximum range of China's farthest reaching conventional ballistic missile is 1,770 km, giving the PLA strategic missile force's (2nd Artillery) extensive reach in Greater Central Asia. In accordance with the PLAAF's evolving doctrine, the strategic missile forces should be used to supplement the PLAAF, which may lack the capability of safely destroying targets that are well defended or have large surface areas.[88] The 2nd Artillery's conventional missiles, as well as PLA regular army tactical missile units, would be employed in both offensive missions and defensive counter attack operations against enemy air bases and support facilities, with the goal of maintaining or regaining the initiative respectively.[89]

The PLA's military doctrine has also evolved. This new approach is a stark contrast to the Maoist "Peoples' War" doctrine, which emphasized leading the enemy into the heartland of China, where it would be destroyed by the masses using both conventional and unconventional tactics. The new doctrine calls for fully integrated forces capable of combined arms force projection beyond China's borders to defend the PRC and its interests. Furthermore, RMA-based doctrine is much more flexible; the PLA often uses its multinational training exercises as a way of getting current doctrine critiqued by foreign commanders while utilizing the experience of their foreign counterparts to gain new approaches to warfare in the 21st century.[90]

PRC analysts have been closely observing COIN operations around the world, especially the U.S. effort in Afghanistan and the Russian operations in the North Caucasus. It seems that many in the PLA favor the U.S. approach to counterinsurgency over the Russian one, preferring the Americans' high-tech reconnaissance and information analysis over the more blunt approach taken by Moscow.[91] China's key observations of U.S. operations have been that air power is an important power projection tool, and unmanned aerial systems (UAS) are a dynamic part of air power, as well as the lesson that information analysis and joint operations are central to modern warfare.[92] China attaches great significance to the gathering, processing, and sharing of intelligence and is moving towards a network-centric approach to COIN.[93] Chinese special forces have used UAS since the 1990s, and the PLA closely follows developments in the field. The PRC has also developed its own drone with offensive capabilities, the CH-3.[94] The PAP has primary responsibility for counterterrorism and COIN operations, suggesting that the Chinese see these activities as primarily domestic in nature, but it still holds that the PLA would play a dominant role in any external operations.[95] In sum, China's conception of COIN has been heavily influenced by what it has seen in Afghanistan, and one should expect to see China attempt to mimic successful U.S. strategies should it ever find itself in a similar counterinsurgency situation.

LACK OF INTENT

Despite China's obvious capability to send a military force into Central Asia, there are a number of reasons to suspect that it will not do so. The PRC remains politically constrained in its actions. Central Asian governments are suspicious of growing Chinese power, as are the citizens of these countries. Nor do Central Asian militaries trust their eastern counterparts. Russia, as well, has an interest in keeping the PLA at bay in what Moscow views as its "near abroad." China is not diplomatically inclined to intervene in Central Asia. Beijing's strategy, as noted previously, is to increase Central Asia's stability through economic growth, and part of the reason for this hands-off, low-interference approach is China's concern about being perceived as belligerent. The PRC's leaders understand that the nations of Central Asia have well-founded suspicions about Beijing's growing power and strive to diffuse such concerns through their cautious diplomacy.[96] China wants to challenge the pervasive negative perceptions that Central Asians have towards it, with the goal of making Chinese power more palatable for them.[97] Beijing does not care what regime is in power in a particular country, as long as that regime will work with it. Unless an extremist government takes power in one of the Central Asian states, these countries will likely not stop cooperating with Beijing on matters of mutual interest.

Central Asian militaries remain much closer to Russia in terms of training and doctrine. [98] The PLA is also not a "natural" military partner for the Central Asian armed forces, which have common ancestry with the Russian military, and they retain many of the same doctrines, equipment, and command structures.

In addition, Russia is responsible for training Central Asia's officer corps and has significant ties to Central Asian militaries outside of the SCO, something which China lacks. The status of Russian as the *lingua franca* of Central Asia also has significant practical implications in the realm of military cooperation.[99] As a result, Russia has a military advantage in the region that will be difficult for China to displace. Central Asians generally prefer to fall within Russia's military shield, rather than China's.[100] Kyrgyzstan and Tajikistan, the two states most likely to experience crises requiring foreign intervention, especially depend on Russia; recall that Kyrgyzstan requested Russian intervention during the 2010 ethnic violence, and Tajikistan still hosts Russian troops on its soil. The PRC has supported Uzbekistan's efforts to prevent such changes from occurring.[101] For example, China and Uzbekistan played a role in blocking Russia from intervening in Kyrgyzstan's ethnic violence during the summer of 2010, despite Kyrgyzstan's request for an intervention and Russia's seeming willingness to do so.[102]

For its part, the PRC remains focused on economic diplomacy and does not seem interested in sending troops to Central Asia; it would rather build up an international image of Beijing as a beneficent neighbor, focused merely on providing security and stability. In Afghanistan, Iran, North Korea, and elsewhere, Beijing has preferred to free ride on the security contributions of other countries. Chinese analysts recognize that, on balance, they have benefited from the U.S military efforts in Central Asia and Afghanistan since, unlike many other countries, the PRC has not had to make a major contribution to support it. Whereas American pressure has induced many of Afghanistan's neighbors to grant the Pentagon military bases and transit rights and has led many other countries to provide combat forces for the unpopular Afghan campaign, China has been able to benefit from these military exertions without having to contribute to them. PRC officials have resisted U.S. and NATO pressure to contribute combat forces to the UN's International Security Assistance Force (ISAF), send police trainers to Kabul, or allow the Pentagon to send military supplies to Afghanistan through Chinese territory. The main weakness with China's regional strategy is its dependence on the foreign forces to hold Central Asian terrorism at bay and preserve a benign investment climate for Chinese investment and trade. If Russia and NATO forces fail at these tasks, then the PRC government might well have to intervene to protect its large geopolitical and growing economic stake in Central Asia.

There are very few circumstances in the current geopolitical climate in which China would engage in armed conflict with any nation along its western border. Although the PLA garrison in Xinjiang Military Region is both qualitatively and quantitatively superior to its neighboring states due to the flexibility and high mobility of its new mechanized divisions,[103] it is unlikely that the PRC would risk its current standing in the region by taking up interventionist policies in all but the most dire circumstances. In most cases, China would feel its interests better served if Russia or the United States dealt with insurgent or ethnic conflict in the GCA region.[104] In the past, border disputes have led to military tensions such as the Sino-Indian wars in the 1970s and disputes with Kyrgyzstan; however, the CCP would not likely risk seeming like a belligerent power and only commit forces in the event of a major threat to Chinese strategic interests. Three circumstances that would threaten these strategic interests and result in the use of Chinese military power include (1) evidence of Central Asian state sponsorship of the "three evils" directed against China; (2) a major risk to China's energy or resource security; or (3) the failure of a neighboring state, which would bring a variety of adverse effects, ranging from arms trafficking into China to humanitarian crises. In this latter case, the PLA might engage the situation multilaterally with the assistance of SCO partner countries because these challenges would not be limited to China alone. A threat to China's energy security could trigger unilateral action due to China's dependence on energy to sustain its economic growth.

ENDNOTES - CHAPTER 4

1. Stephen Blank, "The Central Asian Dimension of Chinese Military Strategy," Washington, DC: The Jamestown Foundation, China Brief Vol. 4, No. 10, 2004, available from *www.jamestown. org/single/?no_cache=1&tx_ttnews[tt_news]=3652*.

2. Pan Guang, "East Turkestan Terrorism and the Terrorist Arc: China's Post-9/11 Anti-Terror Strategy," *The China and Eurasia Forum Quarterly*, Vol. 4, No. 2, 2006, pp. 19-24.

3. Andrew McGregor, "Chinese Counter-Terrorist Strike in Xinjiang," *CACI Analyst*, March 7 2007.

4. Kurt M. Campbell, Nirav Patel, and Richard Weitz, *The Ripple Effect: China's Responses to the Iraq War*, Washington, DC: Center for a New American Security, October 2008, p. 22.

5. Kathleen Moore, "Central Asia: China's Mounting Influence, Part 4—Facing Militant Threats," *Radio Free Europe/Radio Liberty*, November 18, 2004.

6. *Ibid.*

7. Pan Guang, "China and Central Asia: Charting a New Course for Regional Cooperation," *China Brief*, Vol. 7, No. 3, Washington, DC: The Jamestown Foundation, February 7, 2007, available from *www.jamestown.org/single/?no_cache=1&tx_ ttnews%5Btt_news%5D=32468*.

8. *Ibid.*

9. Russell Ong, "China's Security Interests in Central Asia," *Central Asian Survey*, Vol. 24, No. 4, December 2005, p. 432.

10. "China Plans Rail Link to Central Asia for Oil," January 1, 2008, available from *business.uzreport.com/mir.cgi?lan=e&id=42174*.

11. Zhao Huaheng, "China, Russia, and the United States: Prospects for Cooperation in Central Asia," *CEF Quarterly, The Journal of the China-Eurasia Forum*, February 2005, p. 20. available from *www.silkroadstudies.org/new/docs/CEF/CEF_Quarterly_ Winter_2005.doc.pdf*.

12. Marat Yermukanov, "Global and Regional Aspects of Sino-Kyrgyz Cooperation," *CEF Quarterly: The Journal of the China-Eurasia Forum*, October 2004, pp. 13-16.

13. Chinese-Kyrgyz military cooperation is reviewed in Elizabeth Wishnick, *Strategic Consequences of the Iraq War: U.S. Security Interests in Central Asia Reassessed*, Carlisle, PA: Strategic Studies Institute, U.S. Army War College, May 2004, p. 28.

14. Matthew Oresman, "Engaging China in Central Asia," *CEF Monthly*, April/May 2004.

15. "Joint Military Drill to Boost Peace and Stability," *People's Daily Online*, July 21, 2009, available from *english.people.com. cn/90001/90780/91345/6705902.htm*.

16. Joshua Kucera, "Central Asia & Caucasus: Governments Spending Heavily on Arms," *Eurasianet.org*, March 23, 2010, available from *www.eurasianet.org/departments/business/articles/ eav032410.shtml*.

17. Cited in "Beijing Mulls Central Asian Military Deployment," *China Reform Monitor*, June 20, 2005.

18. For more on the Russian reaction to the possibility of China's establishing a military base in Central Asia, see Dmitri Trenin, "Russia and the Shanghai Cooperation Organization: A Difficult Match," *CEF Quarterly: The Journal of the China-Eurasia Forum*, July 2005, p. 26.

19. "Kyrgyzstan Won't Have Chinese Military Base on it Territory," ITAR-TASS News Agency, July 29, 2005. Evidence of possible Chinese interest in establishing such bases, and Russia's presumed opposition to such a development, is discussed in Stephen Blank, "China Joins the Great Central Asian Base Race," *EurasiaNet*, November 15, 2005, available from *www.eurasianet. org/departments/insight/articles/eav111605.shtml*.

20. "Foreign Ministry Spokesperson Jiang Yu's Regular Press Conference on April 8, 2010," PRC Ministry of Foreign Affairs, available from *www.fmprc.gov.cn/eng/xwfw/s2510/t678446.htm*.

21. Jacqueline Newmyer, "The Revolution in Military Affairs with Chinese Characteristics," *Journal of Strategic Studies*, Vol. 33, No. 4, 2010, pp. 483-504.

22. *China's New Great Leap Forward: High Technology and Military Power in the Next Half-Century*, Cicero, IN: Hudson Institute, 2005.

23. Blank, "The Central Asian Dimension of Chinese Military Strategy."

24. Martin Andrew, "The Influence of U.S. Counterinsurgency Operations in Afghanistan on the People's Liberation Army," Andrew Scobell, David Lai, and Roy Kamphausen, eds., *Chinese Lessons from Other People's Wars*, Carlisle, PA: Strategic Studies Institute, U.S. Army War College, November 2011, p. 238, *available from www.strategicstudiesinstitute.army.mil/pubs/display. cfm?pubID=1090*.

25. Blank, "The Central Asian Dimension of Chinese Military Strategy."

26. B. Raman, "Stride 2009 - China's Largest Ever Long-Range Military Exercise," South Asia Analysis Group, August 13, 2009, available from *www.southasiaanalysis. org/%5Cpapers34%5Cpaper3354.html*.

27. Blank, "The Central Asian Dimension of Chinese Military Strategy."

28. Andrew, "The Influence of U.S. Counterinsurgency Operations in Afghanistan on the People's Liberation Army."

29. *Ibid.*

30. "Upgraded Il-76 Plane to Make Maiden Flight in Summer," *RIA Novosti*, March 2, 2012, available from *en.rian.ru/mlitary_news/20120302/171691313.html*.

31. "AC313 is Z8F-100," China Defense Blog, March 18, 2010, available from *china-defense.blogspot.com/2010/03/ac330-is-z-8f-100.html*.

32. Roger McDermott, "PLA Displays Network-Centric Capabilities in Peace Mission 2010," Washington, DC: The Jamestown Foundation, *Eurasia Daily Monitor*, Vol. 7, No. 180, 2010, available from *www.jamestown.org/programs/edm/single/?tx_ttnews[tt_news]=37001&cHash=ff5fd5240d*.

33. Christina Lin, "The PLA's 'Orient Express': Militarization of the Iron Silk Road," Washington, DC: The Jamestown Foundation, China Brief Vol. 11, No. 5, March 25, 2011, available from *www.jamestown.org/programs/chinabrief/single/?tx_ttnews[tt_news]=37698&tx_ttnews[backPid]=25&cHash=61811bad52f8e3abdee dcd41e16bc5c1*.

34. Joshua Kucera, "China, What's Next? Central Asia," *The Diplomat*, available from *the-diplomat.com/whats-next-china/central-asia/*.

35. Roger McDermott, "China Showcases Expeditionary Military Power in Peace Mission 2010," Washington, DC: The Jamestown Foundation, *Eurasia Daily Monitor*, Vol. 7, No. 174, September 28, 2010, available from *www.jamestown.org/single/?no_cache=1&tx_ttnews[tt_news]=36955*.

36. Robert O. Modarelli III, "PLA Missions in Frontier Security and Counterterrorism," Andrew Scobell, David Lai and Roy Kamphausen, eds., *Beyond the Strait: PLA Missions other than Taiwan*, Carlisle, PA: Strategic Studies Institute, U.S. Army War College, April 2009, p. 142, available from *www.strategicstudies institute.army.mil/pubs/display.cfm?pubid=910*.

37. "PLA Helicopter S&R Operations." China Defense Blog, August 17, 2010, available from *china-defense.blogspot.com/2010/08/pla-helicopter-s-operations.html*.

38. Yu Bin, "Learning from the Neighbors: The Peoples' Liberation Army Examines the Small Wars and Counterinsurgencies Waged by Russia," Andrew Scobell, David Lai, and Roy Kamphausen, eds., *Chinese Lessons from Other People's Wars*, Carlisle, PA: Strategic Studies Institute, U.S. Army War College, November 2011, p. 286, available from *www.strategicstudiesinstitute.army.mil/pubs/display.cfm?pubID=1090*.

39. *Ibid.*

40. "Sino-Russian Military Drills Demonstrate Commitment to World Peace," *People's Daily Online*, August 19, 2005, available from *www.politicalaffairs.net/article/view/1695/1/114/*.

41. Vladimir Mukhin, "Po uyguro-chechenskomu stsenariyu" ("On the Uighur-Chechen Scenario"), *Nezavisimyay Gazeta*, July 21, 2009, available from *www.ng.ru/politics/2009-07-21/2_uchenia.html*.

42. *Ibid.*; and "Russia and China: Joint Military Exercises: Comment and Analysis from Taipei, London, Singapore and Tokyo," *WorldPress.org*, August 26, 2005, available from *www.worldpress.org/Asia/2138.cfm*.

43. "U.S. is Watching Russia-China Drill," *New York Times*, August 19, 2005, available from *www.nytimes.com/2005/08/18/world/asia/18iht-exercise.html?_r=1*.

44. Sergei Blagov, "Russian-Chinese War Game Meant to Boost Bilateral Partnership," *Eurasia Daily Monitor*, August 18,

2005, available from *www.jamestown.org/single/?no_cache=1&tx_ttnews[tt_news]=30804*.

45. Jason Kelly, "Anti-Terrorism with Chinese Characteristics: Peace Mission 2007 in Context," *China Brief*, October 31, 2007, available from *www.jamestown.org/single/?no_cache=1&tx_ttnews%5Btt_news%5D=4514*.

46. Zhang Quanyi, "Aims of Sino-Russian Military Exercises," *UPI*, July 23, 2009, available from *www.upiasia.com/Security/2009/07/23/aims_of_sino-russian_military_exercises/8829/*.

47. "Mission for Peace Targets Terrorists," *CCTV*, July 23, 2009, available from *english.cctv.com/20090723/106704.shtml*.

48. Peng Kuang and Li Xiaokun, "Sino-Russian Drill to Begin Despite Crash," *China Daily*, July 22, 2009.

49. Taonan tactics training base is one of the PLA's major bases for military exercises. It belongs to the PLA's Shenyang Military Command, which borders Russia's Far Eastern region to the north.

50. Liu Anqi, ed., "Day 2 of China-Russia Anti-Terror Drill," *CCTV*, July 24, 2009, available from *www.cctv.com/program/newshour/20090724/104689.shtml*.

51. "Russian Troops Go Aboard Train to Take Part in Chinese Exercises," *Itar-Tass*, July 8, 2009.

52. Zhang Ning, "Chinese Army Battle Group Ready for Russia-China Joint Military Exercise," *CCTV*, July 20, 2009, available from *www.cctv.com/program/newshour/20090720/104771.shtml*.

53. "First Contingent of Chinese Soldiers Arrive in Kazakhstan for SCO Drills," *Xinhua*, September 7, 2010, available from *news.xinhuanet.com/english2010/china/2010-09/07/c_13483072.htm*.

54. "SCO Anti-Terrorist Drills to Show SCO Potential in Security Area," *Itar-Tass*, September 10, 2010, available from *www.itar-tass.com/eng/level2.html?NewsID=15480561&PageNum=0*.

55. "SCO Troops Stage Second Joint Training," *Xinhua*, September 16, 2010.

56. Liang Jun, "Three Highlights of 'Peace Mission 2010' Worth Expecting," *People's Daily Online*, September 13, 2010, available from *english.people.com.cn/90001/90776/90883/7138773. html*.

57. "Kazakh Official Calls for United Efforts," *China Daily*, September 11, 2010, available from *english.cri. cn/6966/2010/09/11/2481s594022.htm*.

58. "SCO to Begin Large-Scale Anti-Terror Drills in Kazakhstan," *RIA Novosti*, September 9, 2010, available from *en.rian.ru/ mlitary_news/20100909/160523960.html*; and "SCO Anti-Terrorist Drills to Show SCO Potential in Security Area."

59. "SCO to Begin Large-Scale Anti-Terror Drills in Kazakhstan."

60. "Chinese Troops Pay Attention to Coordination with Friendly Forces," *Xinhua*, September 19, 2010, available from *english.cri.cn/6909/2010/09/19/1461s595271.htm*.

61. Ding Ying, "Practicing for Peace," *Beijing Review*, September 21, 2010, available from *www.bjreview.com.cn/quotes/txt/2010-09/21/content_299532.htm*.

62. "SCO to Begin Large-Scale Anti-Terror Drills in Kazakhstan."

63. Ding Ying.

64. Roger N. McDermott, *The Rising Dragon: SCO Peace Mission 2007*, Washington, DC: Jamestown Foundation, October 2007, available from *www.jamestown.org/uploads/media/Jamestown-McDermottRisingDragon.pdf*.

65. "Chinese Troops Pay Attention to Coordination with Friendly Forces."

66. "First Contingent of Chinese Soldiers Arrive in Kazakhstan for SCO Drills."

67. Ding Ying.

68. "Chinese Army Hones Transportation Skills at SCO War Games," *Xinhua*, September 22, 2010, available from *news.xinhuanet.com/english2010/china/2010-09/22/c_13525299.htm.*

69. See *www.gzt.ru/topnews/politics/.*

70. Liang Jun, "Three highlights of 'Peace Mission 2010' worth expecting."

71. McDermott, "PLA Displays Network-Centric Capabilities in Peace Mission 2010."

72. Ding Ying.

73. Gabe Collins, "China's Military Gets Expeditionary," *The Diplomat,* April 15, 2011, available from *the-diplomat.com/2011/04/15/china%E2%80%99s-military-gets-expeditionary/?all=true.*

74. Wilson Chun Hei Chau, "Explaining China's Participation in Bilateral and Multilateral Military Exercises," *Security Challenges*, Vol. 7, No. 3, pp. 51-69.

75. McDermott, "China Showcases Expeditionary Military Power in Peace Mission 2010."

76. Roger Cliff, Rand Corporation, and Project Air Force, "Shaking the Heavens and Splitting the Earth: Chinese Air Force Employment Concepts in the 21st Century," Santa Monica, CA: RAND, p. 50, available from *public.eblib.com/EBLPublic/PublicView.do?ptiID=669770.*

77. Blank, "The Central Asian Dimension of Chinese Military Strategy."

78. Martin Andrew, "Guarding the West: China's New Mechanized Infantry Division," *China Brief,* Vol. 7, No. 10, 2007.

79. "Jian-11 Multirole Fighter Aircraft," *Sino Defence*, available from *www.sinodefence.com/airforce/fighter/j11.asp*.

80. "Su-30MKK Multirole Fighter Aircraft," *Sino Defence*, available from *www.sinodefence.com/airforce/fighter/su30.asp*.

81. "Hong-6U Tanker," *Sino Defence,* available from *www.sino-defence.com/airforce/airlift/h6tanker.asp*.

82. Cliff, "Shaking the Heavens and Splitting the Earth," p. 50.

83. "Hong-6 Bomber" *Sino Defence*, available from *www.sinodefence.com/airforce/airlift/*.

84. Cliff, "Shaking the Heavens and Splitting the Earth."

85. "IL-76MD Transport Aircraft," *Sino Defence*, available from *www.sinodefence.com/airforce/airlift/il76.asp*.

86. "Yun-9 Multipurpose," *Sino Defence,* available from *www.sinodefence.com/airforce/airlift/y9.asp*.

87. Cliff, "Shaking the Heavens and Splitting the Earth."

88. *Ibid.,* p. 74.

89. *Ibid.,* p. 134.

90. Chau, pp. 51-69.

91. Yu Bin, p. 278.

92. Andrew, "The Influence of U.S. Counterinsurgency Operations in Afghanistan on the People's Liberation Army," pp. 240-241.

93. Yu Bin, pp. 309-310.

94. Andrew, "The Influence of U.S. Counterinsurgency Operations in Afghanistan on the People's Liberation Army," pp. 244-246.

95. Modarelli, "PLA Missions in Frontier Security and Counterterrorism," pp. 148-152.

96. Adiljan Umarov and Dmitriy Pashkun, "Tensions in Sino-Central Asian Relations and their Implications for Regional Security," Central Asia Series, Vol. 6, No. 2, Conflict Studies Research Center, 2006, p. 15, available from *www.isn.ethz.ch/isn/Digital-Library/Publications/Detail/?ots591=0c54e3b3-1e9c-be1e-2c24-a6a8c7060233&lng=en&id=92580*.

97. Stephen Aris, Eurasian *Regionalism: The Shanghai Cooperation Organization*, New York: Palgrave Macmillan, 2011, pp. 77-78.

98. Sebastien Peyrouse, "Military Cooperation between China and Central Asia: Breakthroughs, Limits, and Prospects," China Brief, Vol. 10, No. 5, 2010, available from *www.jamestown.org/programs/chinabrief/single/?tx_ttnews[tt_news]=36123&tx_ttnews[backPid]=25&cHash=42beea809e*.

99. *Ibid.*

100. Umarov and Pashkun, "Tensions in Sino-Central Asian Relations and their Implications for Regional Security," p. 10.

101. Richard Weitz, "Military Exercises Underscore the SCO's Character," *CACI Analyst*, May 25, 2011, available from *cacianalyst.org/?q=node/5565*.

102. Stephen Blank, "A Sino-Uzbek Axis in Central Asia?" *CACI Analyst*, September 1, 2010, available from *www.cacianalyst.org/?q=node/5395*.

103. Martin Andrew, "Guarding the West: China's New Mechanized Infantry Division," *China Brief*, Vol. 7, No. 10, 2007.

104. Olga Oliker, Thomas S. Szayna, and RAND Corporation, "Faultlines of Conflict in Central Asia and the South Caucasus: Implications for the U.S. Army," Santa Monica, CA: RAND, 2002, p. 216.

ABOUT THE CONTRIBUTORS

STEPHEN J. BLANK served as the Strategic Studies Institute's expert on the Soviet block and the post-Soviet world from 1989 to 2013. Prior to that he was Associate Professor of Soviet Studies at the Center for Aerospace Doctrine, Research, and Education, Maxwell Air Force Base, AL; and taught at the University of Texas, San Antonio, and at the University of California, Riverside. Dr. Blank is the editor of *Imperial Decline: Russia's Changing Position in Asia*, coeditor of *Soviet Military and the Future*, and author of *The Sorcerer as Apprentice: Stalin's Commissariat of Nationalities, 1917-1924*. He has also written many articles and conference papers on Russia, the Commonwealth of Independent States, and Eastern European security issues. Dr. Blank's current research deals with proliferation and the revolution in military affairs, and energy and security in Eurasia. His two most recent books are *Russo-Chinese Energy Relations: Politics in Command* London, UK: Global Markets Briefing, 2006; and *Natural Allies? Regional Security in Asia and Prospects for Indo-American Strategic Cooperation*, Carlisle, PA: Strategic Studies Institute, U.S. Army War College, 2005. Dr. Blank holds a B.A. in history from the University of Pennsylvania, and an M.A. and Ph.D. in history from the University of Chicago.

ARIEL COHEN is Senior Research Fellow in Russian and Eurasian Studies and International Energy Policy at the Katherine and Shelby Cullom Davis Institute for International Policy at The Heritage Foundation. He directs high-level conferences on Eurasian security, terrorism and energy, the rule of law, crime and corruption, and a variety of other issues. He also directs

Heritage's energy simulation exercises and war games involving Russia (2007-11). Dr. Cohen conducts White House briefings and regularly lectures for the U.S. Government, including the Foreign Service Institute of the U.S. Department of State, the Joint Chiefs of Staff, and the Training and Doctrine and Special Forces Commands of the U.S. armed services, Central Intelligence Agency, and Defense Intelligence Agency. He frequently testifies before committees of the U.S. Congress, including the Senate and House Foreign Relations Committees, the House Armed Services Committee, the House Judiciary Committee, and the Helsinki Commission. Dr. Cohen is also a Member of the Council of Foreign Relations and International Institute for Strategic Studies (London). Dr. Cohen authored *Russian Imperialism: Development and Crisis* (Praeger Publishers/Greenwood, 1996 and 1998), edited and co-authored *Eurasia in Balance*, (Ashgate, United Kingdom, 2005), and authored *Kazakhstan: The Road to Independence: Energy Policy and the Birth of a Nation* (School of Advanced International Studies, Johns Hopkins Central Asia Caucasus Institute, 2008).

GEIR FLIKKE is Professor II at the High North Center for Business and Governance in Bodø, Norway. He is a member of the Advisory Board of the Czech journal, *Defence and Strategy*. Previous appointments were as Associate Professor at the Institute for Literature, Areas Studies, and European Languages, University of Oslo; Adjunct Professor at the Norwegian Institute of International Affairs (NUPI); teaching part-time at the University of Oslo; Senior Researcher, Research Fellow, and Assistant Director (Acting Director at NUPI); and as Political Advisor, Parliamentary group, The Conservative Party. Professor Flikke has completed the project RuBeKa2 (a comparison of the employment of workers' rights in Russia, Kazakhstan, and Belarus) and works on questions related to Russia's modernization process in the north. He has participated in a workshop on European security. Professor Flikke is the author of an article entitled "Eastward Bound: Options and Limitations in the Union's Eastern Policies"; and has written a chapter in the book, *Arctic Security in an Age of Climate Change* (University of Cambridge, James Kraska). Professor Flikke holds a D.Arts. from the University of Oslo (Thesis: The Failure of a Movement: The Rise and Decline of Democratic Russia 1989-1992) and is a candidate in philosophy from the University of Oslo.

RICHARD WEITZ is Senior Fellow and Director of the Center for Political-Military Analysis at Hudson Institute. His current research includes regional security developments relating to Europe, Eurasia, and East Asia, as well as U.S. foreign, defense, and homeland security policies. Dr. Weitz also is a nonresident Senior Advisor at the Project on National Security Reform where he oversees case study research; he is also a nonresident Senior Fellow at the Center for a New American Security where he contributes to various defense projects. Dr. Weitz has published or edited several books and monographs, including *The Russian Military Today and Tomorrow* (2010); *Global Security Watch-Russia* (2009); a volume of *National Security Case Studies* (2008); *China-Russia Security Relations* (2008); *Kazakhstan and the New International Politics of Eurasia* (2008); *Mismanaging Mayhem: How Washington Responds to Crisis* (2008); *The Reserve Policies of Nations: A Comparative Analysis* (2007); and *Revitalising US-Russian Security Cooperation: Practical Measures* (2005).

www.ingramcontent.com/pod-product-compliance
Lightning Source LLC
Chambersburg PA
CBHW070707290526
45790CB00001B/483